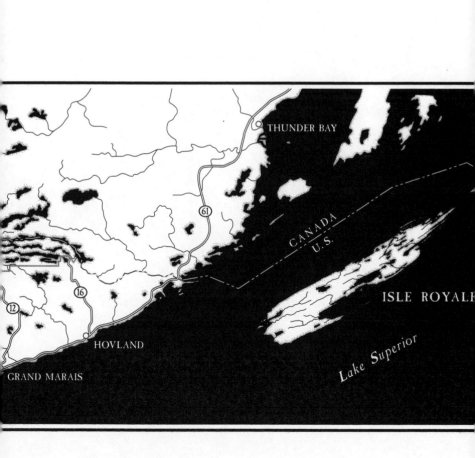

Boundary
Waters

The Grace
of the Wild

PAUL GRUCHOW

MILKWEED
EDITIONS

Published 1997 by Milkweed Editions
Printed in the United States of America
Cover design by Adrian Morgan, Red Letter Design
Cover and endsheet photos by Jim Brandenburg
Interior design by Will Powers
Interior illustrations by Matt Kania
Literature for a Land Ethic woodcut by Betsy Bowen
The text of this book is set in Trump Mediaeval.
97 98 99 00 01   5 4 3 2 1
First Edition

Some of the material in this book was originally published in *Travels in Canoe Country* (Boston: Little, Brown and Company, 1992). Text copyright © 1992 by Paul Gruchow. Reprinted by permission of Bulfinch.

Milkweed Editions is a not-for-profit publisher. Special thanks to Reader's Legacy underwriters Elly and Sheldon Sturgis and Medora Woods. We also gratefully acknowledge support from the Elmer L. and Eleanor J. Andersen Foundation; Target Stores, Dayton's, and Mervyn's by the Dayton Hudson Foundation; Wallace and Mary Lee Dayton; Doherty, Rumble, and Butler Foundation; General Mills Foundation; Honeywell Foundation; Jerome Foundation; The McKnight Foundation; Andrew W. Mellon Foundation; Minnesota State Arts Board through an appropriation by the Minnesota State Legislature; Challenge and Literature Programs of the National Endowment for the Arts; Kate and Stuart Nielsen; Lawrence and Elizabeth Ann O'Shaughnessy Charitable Income Trust in honor of Lawrence M. O'Shaughnessy; Piper Jaffray Companies, Inc.; Ritz Foundation; John and Beverly Rollwagen Fund of the Minneapolis Foundation; The St. Paul Companies, Inc.; Star Tribune/Cowles Media Foundation; James R. Thorpe Foundation; and generous individuals.

Library of Congress Cataloging-in-Publication Data

Gruchow, Paul.
    Boundary waters : the grace of the wild / Paul Gruchow. — 1st ed.
        p.   cm.
    ISBN 1-57131-211-0
    1. Natural history—Minnesota—Boundary Waters Canoe Area.
2. Canoes and canoeing—Minnesota—Boundary Waters Canoe Area.
3. Natural history—Superior, Lake, Region.   4. Gruchow, Paul.
I. Title.
QH105.M55G78   1997
508.776'7—dc21   96–52086
                                                                  CIP

This book is printed on acid-free paper.

*This book is for Marjorie Fader,
who was there in bright days,
and for Elizabeth Umphrey,
who was there in dark ones.*

Boundary Waters

Acknowledgments

The essay, "The Grace of the Wild," here makes its second appearance in print in book form. The essay served earlier as the text for a volume of Gerald Brimacombe's photographs, *Travels in Canoe Country*. Like many writers, I have been attracted to the idea that a marriage of text and photographs would result in a whole larger than the sum of its parts. The truth, unfortunately, seems to be that the photographs in such collections inevitably overwhelm the words. Since the words in *Travels in Canoe Country* were meant to be read, I am pleased to be able to offer them in this quieter and more accessible setting.

Portions of "Walking the Border" first appeared in *Minnesota Monthly*; the whole essay, much revised, appears here for the first time. The other two essays in this book are also new. "By Light of the Winter Moon" is based on a real experience, but I have invented both the names and the biographical details of the students in order to protect the privacy of the real ones. "Wild Isle" first appeared in *Ascent*, volume 21, number 2. I was felicitously joined at various times on my trips to Isle Royale by John Scholl, Gary Deason, Matt Nielson, and Andrew Gamson.

I am grateful to Nancy, Laura, and Aaron Gruchow for tolerating with grace and understanding the absences these journeys have required; to Emilie Buchwald for her support, personal as well as editorial, without which I could not have managed the task; to Beth Olson for her careful attention to the details; to the staff of Milkweed Editions, who care about making good books; to my friends Lou Martinelli, Richard Levins, and Jonathon Larson, who are there when I need to talk; to Daniel Kelly and Bonnie Blodgett, an editor and an agent who helped me to find my way; to Betty Savage, who provided me with valuable materials about Isle Royale, including a rare copy of the report of the Michigan Geological Survey's expedition to the islands in 1904–05; and to Gerald Brimacombe who first encouraged me to write about the north country.

Preface

I feel, I confess, like an impostor when I write about the canoe country of northern Minnesota, a classically beautiful landscape that has had more than its share of interpreters and has been photographed so often as to have become, like the Matterhorn or the stone heads of Easter Island or the Eiffel Tower, a visual cliché. Many thousands of people know this landscape better than I and probably love it more. I grew up on prairies and took at first sight to deserts, peatlands, alpine tundra, and the shallow waters of oceans, but the canoe country was, for me, an acquired taste.

I am, moreover, a poor swimmer and afraid, therefore, of being in boats. An inept canoeist who has been unable to master even the basic J stroke, I am the sort of canoeist sophisticates joke about having encountered on their own suave passages through the water wilderness: "You ought to have seen him, the bow of his boat halfway out of the water, paddling like a madman, first on this side of the canoe and then on that side, stroking like a windmill, and weaving all over the lake as if he were running a slalom!" I can hear the laughter because I have joined in it a time or two myself on an occasion when I hadn't the courage to confess my own naïveté.

In fact, the very first trip I made into the canoe country, rather late in life given that I am both a Minnesotan and a naturalist, was a solo one—no doubt quite insane—a journey I undertook alone because I was too embarrassed by my extreme ignorance of all things having to do with water to be seen by anybody who might be willing to join me. The learning curve on that occasion was, as it is said, steep, but I survived; I suppose that is one important reason why I keep going back. I have even, since then, done so in company, most memorably with my son Aaron—who has almost forgiven me for tipping him without warning or good cause into an icy lake—and, on other occasions, with my neighbor and colleague, Gary Deason, whose deep love of the canoe country has been infectious and instructive and who has endured the consequences of my incompetence—as, for example, when I maneuvered us into a backwards run down a rapids—with such grace as only a friend, and a very patient one at that, could summon.

The other companion who figures in these pages, as he has in those of three previous books, is John Scholl, with whom I have undertaken a long walk nearly every summer for the last fifteen years, and who has had to endure not only the many occasions when I, with my unerringly mistaken sense of direction, have led us both astray but also my incorrigible habit of writing in public about our private adventures. He is the perfect walking companion: competent in all things, long-suffering, affable in adversity, calm in times of danger, interested in everything, and immune to the tedium and boredom that are an inevitable part of every long journey under one's own power. I could not have written any of my books without John because it was he who taught me how to be in the out-of-doors.

There is no disgrace—I have finally come to appreciate in the shoals of middle age—in needing teachers, and I know how fortunate I have been in the excellence of mine. I am pretty certain, too, that I am not the world's only klutz. I know that this condition has not kept me from the exceedingly deep joy of being in wild places. If I write about the aches and pains, the fears, the frustrations of wilderness travel, it is only to emphasize that I myself am no master of the subject. As I have blundered my way around the canoe country, so I have climbed mountains only to be miserably sick at every summit; have walked thousands of miles, but at a pace that would make a serious hiker blush; have dived and snorkeled among coral reefs certain that I was about to drown at any moment; have slept out in wild places, often alone, hundreds of nights of my life, one of them spent in abject terror of the intruder rustling about just beyond my tent, which proved in the weak light of dawn to have been a quite small box turtle; have fallen, stumbled, and hobbled about; have been lost, lonely, cold to the core, dangerously overheated, blistered and feverish. I am not strong, nor well-conditioned, nor physically adept, nor fearless, but I am stubborn and curious and, despite my inadequacies, most of the happiest moments of my life have been spent in nature. I would think these pages worthwhile if they encouraged even one reader to believe that one does not need fashionable gear or polished technique or the sort of body one likes to show off, shirtless, in the blazing sun of midday in order to venture into the wild. Let others write rapturously about prancing naked through the woods. This book is for the sort of person who, as a kid, was shunted off to the volleyball field at summer camp while the athletic stars vied for the championship in the baseball playoffs.

To many people in the upper Midwest, the term "boundary waters" refers specifically to the approximately two-and-a-half million acres of lands protected by three contiguous wilderness preserves along the Minnesota-Ontario border: Quetico Provincial Park, the Boundary Waters Canoe Area Wilderness, and Voyageurs National Park. Much of the country described in this book lies outside of that area but within the same ecosystem. So I need to explain that when I use the words "boundary waters" in the title, I mean to refer to the whole ecosystem and not just to those parts of it that are under formal protection.

At a congressional hearing on the future of the canoe country a few years ago, a man paraded in front of the school gymnasium where the meeting was to be held with a placard reading, "We Are Pork and Beaners Not L. L. Beaners and Proud of It." I'm a pork and beaner myself and also, without the slightest sense of contradiction, a passionate advocate of wilderness. I believe wilderness to be necessary, if not to the sanity of the culture, at least to my own sanity. Speaking in defense of nature is sometimes characterized as a frivolity, as a preoccupation of those who are afraid of tackling serious issues like poverty and violence, racism and sexism. I would only point out that the same people in the Congress who are busy kicking holes in the social safety net are also those who would sell off the nation's forests for a song, give away its national parks, and trash its wilderness preserves; there is a connection between the two impulses.

Nature is the ultimate humbler, both of persons and of civilizations. It can be destroyed by greed, but it never flatters the greedy; it can, for a time, be made the domain of elites, but it outlives them; it can be temporarily overpowered, but never, except at the peril of all, overwhelmed. On the other hand, nature showers its bountiful blessings upon the mighty and the meek in equal proportion. The howl of a wolf, the cry of a loon, the lap of clean water against an untrammeled shore constitute the only common currency; to defend them is to labor in the most elementary way for the general good.

These essays are offered as a way of applauding the many admirers of the canoe country wilderness who have worked so tirelessly over the last century to defend it against irreversible harm.

NORTHFIELD, MINNESOTA

JANUARY 1997

Boundary Waters

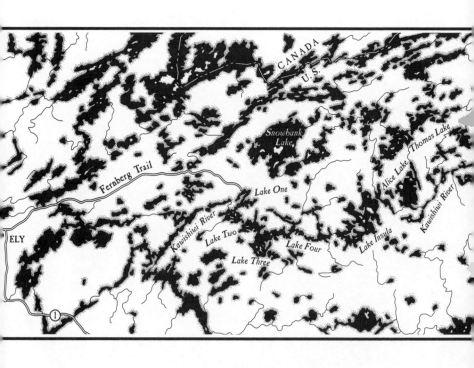

SUMMER

The Grace of the Wild

The Grace
of the Wild

LAUDS

*A Psalm of Praise:
Wilderness Travel
as an Artistic Act*

Being on the move, seeing
what you have never seen
before, not knowing where
you will rest your head
when night falls, receiving
what comes as it comes, expect-
ing everything and nothing: this is
the allure of the canoe country. Every
stroke of the paddle or step along the
trail with a canoe on your
shoulders or a pack on your
back literally enlarges
your world.

You travel under your own power and with the aid
of ancient and elegantly simple tools—the canoe, the
paddle, a pair of boots. Someone was traveling this
way ten thousand years ago, and someone may be
doing the same ten thousand years from now. In a
world where change seems the only constant, where
the past is increasingly suspect and the future ever
more doubtful, it is exhilarating to be in touch with
something that "binds together all humanity—the
dead to the living and the living to the unborn."

The words are Joseph Conrad's, defining the work
of the artist. Every earnest journey into the heart of
the canoe country is, on the same terms, potentially
a work of art, accessible to all.

The thinker, Conrad says, makes an appeal from
ideas, and the scientist from facts. But "the artist ap-
peals to that part of our being which is not dependent
upon wisdom: to that in us which is a gift and not
an acquisition—and, therefore, more permanently
enduring. He speaks to our capacity for delight and
wonder, to the sense of mystery surrounding our
lives; to our sense of pity, and beauty, and pain; to the
latent feeling of fellowship with all creation—and to
the subtle but invincible conviction of solidarity that
knits together the loneliness of innumerable hearts,
to the solidarity in dreams, in joy, in sorrow, in aspi-
rations, in illusions, in hope, in fear, which binds men
to each other, which binds together all humanity—
the dead to the living and the living to the unborn."

A wilderness journey makes just this appeal. It
speaks:

To that part of our being which is not dependent upon wisdom: Not to what we have learned from books, but to whatever depends upon experience with the physical world: knowing how to read a footprint in the mud, how to steer a canoe into the wind, how to make a fire in the rain, what sort of weather the clouds and the wind foretell, where to look for a moose, which of the mushrooms in the forest are edible, whether the sound in the night is sinister or benign, which bird sings overhead, what flower blooms in the marsh.

To that which is a gift and not an acquisition: For nothing one encounters along the way can be possessed beyond the span of a single lifetime, or turned to any monetary advantage that is not destructive, or preserved unchanged for so much as twenty-four hours. Nothing here—not the mists that rise in the morning, nor the wind that blows at midday, nor the curtain of colors that falls in the evening, nor the slap of a beaver's tail in the night—can be commandeered, or caused to happen, or forbidden.

To our capacity for delight and wonder: The water tumbling from one lake into the next, the laughter of loons, the howling of wolves, the waft of cool air upon a sweaty brow, the silence in cedar swamps, the majesty of tall pines, the soaring of eagles, the sudden shimmering of lights in the northern sky at midnight: all these, freely given, daily remind us along the way of the grace abounding in the world.

To the sense of mystery surrounding our lives: The forest floor strewn with bones announces death;

the string of bejeweled butterfly eggs laid out upon
a leaf, the one mystery as large as God, life itself; and
the beating of our own hearts, suddenly audible in
the stillness of a moonless wilderness night, the thin-
ness of the thread that binds the one to the other.

To our sense of pity, and beauty, and pain: Such
old-fashioned words; pity—friendly sympathy, the
desire to deliver mercy—being the most disreputable
of the lot: "The gilded sheath of pity conceals the
dagger of envy," Nietzsche, Conrad's contemporary,
said, expressing the more modern view; and we have,
perhaps, forgotten the connection between beauty
and pain—the words *awful* and *awesome* come from
the same root—until we have all day long battled a
fierce wind blowing out of the west and, at last, with
aching muscles, have made camp in some sheltered
cove, discovering then the bliss that descends with
the silence after the last light.

To the latent feeling of fellowship with all creation: the sudden conviction, arriving in quiet moments, that the pine dancing in the breeze, and the
otter cavorting in the lake, and the loon laughing
in the unseen distance are not aliens after all, but
neighbors, distant, yet potentially knowable, like
the stranger who rides the same bus as you every
morning: Latent because it is, for most of us, a feeling poorly exercised. It comes alive, the Zen master
Dogen reminds us, not because of what we ourselves
experience, but because of all that is experienced
in our presence. "To carry yourself forward and experience myriad things," he said, "is delusion. But

myriad things coming forth and experiencing *them-selves* is awakening."

The journey is indistinct from the traveler. As it is the instrument of awakening, so the traveler is aroused; what stirs is the inner voice of the artist.

MATINS

Daybreak: The Songs of Birds

I waken in canoe country. It is beginning to be light. Birds sing in the forest undergrowth and in the canopy overhead. I stir in my sleeping bag, indulging the luxury of being half-awake but under no compunction to rise, just as I did a long time ago.

A pine cone thuds onto the roof of the tent. Then another. Soon they are plummeting like hailstones. There is no wind, and the cones are too numerous to be falling of their own accord. I am wide awake now. The first light of dawn has penetrated the netting of my tent door. What can be creating this ruckus? Above me, I hear the shrill, angry chattering of a squirrel. I suddenly understand: I, squatting on claimed territory, am admonished, belligerently, to pick up my things and get out.

Chastened, I think of rising. Another bombardment of pine cones hits. But I am still cosseted in my dreams. Shifting positions in my sleeping bag, feeling warm and groggy, I close my eyes, trying to resuscitate the dream I have already half-forgotten.

Since I was a child, I have rarely known mornings like this. "Rise and stomp," my mother would call

every dawn with aggressive cheerfulness, "there's
daylight in the swamp." (I did not know, nor, I think,
did she, that this was a lumberjack's call.) I would
refuse to respond, although usually I was already
half-awake. From the beginning, I rebelled against
authority. But more than cantankerous independence
kept me from obeying. Often I was summoned in the
middle of one of those captivating dream stories that
linger in the half-conscious blush of awakening.
I didn't want to get up until I had finished the story.

People who stayed in bed after sunrise would
never amount to anything, I was told, would never
get on in life. I was a child. What would I have
wanted to amount to? What was there to get on with?

Dreams in themselves were suspect in our house-
hold. We were fundamentalist Christians with a keen
appreciation of self-discipline, and dreams were
something one couldn't control. They were, like lust,
envy, and pride, sins of unbridled passion—passion
was always, in the world of my youth, unbridled, and
anything unbridled meant trouble. I was, worst of all,
a profligate daydreamer. Daydreaming was doubly
sinful, the union of unbridled passion and idleness.
I dreamed, as usual, of grandeur, although of an
odd and contradictory sort. Sometimes I envisioned
becoming a wild man and sometimes a spellbinding
orator, speaking before batteries of microphones to
crowds of transfixed millions. When other Minnesota
boys my age were fantasizing about Harmon
Killebrew, I idolized Billy Graham and Bomba the
Jungle Boy.

I seem to have survived my dreams. I haven't overcome the impulse to preach, but I have lost the delusion that it is of any use, and I have taken more or less satisfactorily to domestication: I don't pee on the carpets, and I use a knife and fork at the dinner table. I sleep too soundly, these days, to remember my nocturnal dreams, and it is, I suppose, a sign of middle age, or of resignation, that I seldom day-dream of glory anymore. I imagine that if a lightning bolt were on the way, it would have struck by now.

In a sense, though, I have made dreaming the work of my life. Writing—any art—happens in a pe-culiar state of mind, more subconscious than deliber-ate, that the handbooks on the subject are always hard-put, and a bit embarrassed, to describe: a kind of trance, it is often said, but really an induced and alert dreaming. When I stayed abed those childhood mornings working out the endings of my dreams, I was rehearsing the work of the storyteller. It has never seemed like real work to me, but we live in a time when labor is expected to be drudgerous and unpleasant, the fifty weeks of servitude that we spend to buy two we hope will be happy.

Accustomed as I am to days of professional reverie, I nevertheless find the vividness of my dream life fully revived only when I have gone into a wilder-ness for a time. One reason, I suppose, is that I sleep then like a child. Because there is not much to do in the woods after the sun has gone down, and because I am pleasantly weary after a day of paddling or hiking, I revert to the bedtimes of childhood, sleeping longer

and at least some of the time less deeply, positioned
to be conscious of my dreams. In the morning, I
awaken not to the clanging of an alarm, but slowly,
naturally. The benefaction of unfettered hours dawns.
I am free again to savor to the finish what my dream-
mind has begun.

And I accept, when I am in the woods, the idea
that I do not completely command my life. To venture into a wilderness is to submit to the authority of
nature. This may also seem a regression—adults command, children submit—but it is actually a progres-
sion toward a higher maturity, one that realizes the
conceit of the enduring human dream of dominion.

Letting go of this dream, even temporarily, un-
stops the wilder and more creative dreams that we
have not had access to since the last time—as children, perhaps—when we expected life to be an endless unfolding of surprises. It is only when we are
prepared to be astonished and confounded that we
are able to dream productively.

Every artist knows how futile the work of the
imagination is until it has been freed to find its own
way. The artist who tries to manufacture inspiration
is frustrated at every turn, and the work that results
is heavy and dull. But the one who tags along after
the dream-line, attentive and open of heart, sometimes finds in the astonishing territory toward which
it leads some treasure worthy of the embrace of
memory.

Henry David Thoreau advocated the tonic of
sauntering, another form of dreamy submission, the

leisurely, meandering gait of the free of heart, who set out upon the road open to every possibility and closed to none. The word *saunter*, Thoreau suggests, in one of his most inspired bits of punning, derives from the pilgrims of the Middle Ages who cast aside everything to wander in search of the *Sainte Terre*, and came thereby to be known as *Sainte-Terrers*: Holy-Landers. "We should go forth on the shortest walk, perchance," Thoreau says, "in the spirit of undying adventure, never to return,—prepared to send back our embalmed hearts only as relics to our desolate kingdom."

On my way into this wilderness, I tarried for a night along its southeastern boundary, Lake Superior's North Shore, where craggy cliffs meet an oceanic expanse of chill, deep, ice-blue water, a coastline worthy of the Pacific or the Atlantic. After dinner, restless and excited about the journey to come, I sauntered along the pebbled beach and out onto a spit of rock, seeking nothing in particular but to idle away an hour.

I admired the fist-sized blue and gray and sometimes black beach stones, rounded and smooth from centuries of churning in the now gentle, now thunderous, ever relentless waves. They seemed fallen and solidified pieces of sky, so much the same color were they as the blues and grays in the distance, where earth and heaven met vaguely, shimmeringly over the lake. I looked into pools of water caught in shallow basins in the polished granite above the beach, arched like a surfacing whale, hoping in vain to encounter some creature staring back at me. I admired the tiny cushion plants blooming in the crevices of rock and the asters making a lavender splash on the leeward side of the spit, where, diverted by it, a river ran its last thousand yards parallel to the shore before finding an opportunity and slipping silently into the Superior. A man and his dog fished just above the bar of the outlet for steelhead trout. The trout seemed not to be biting. The fisherman alternately tended his line and his dog, for whom he now and then tossed a whitened stick of driftwood, which the dog bounded into the current of the river and fetched back, dreaming of what glory? The man, perhaps, fished as Thoreau's neighbors did, "much more in the Walden Pond of their own natures, and baited their hooks with darkness." Overhead, gulls wheeled, crying in the salty voices of the sea that these waters would at last reach in some future century.

The sun setting over the thousand-foot ridge behind me infused the sky with a salmon colored light which echoed in the granite's rosy crystals of quartz. I zipped my jacket against the evening breeze and turned back toward the car. Along the way, I became aware of a slight motion at the periphery of my vision. Pausing to take account of it, I found myself staring into the eyes of two baby mink, their dark coats fuzzy with the fine hair of infancy, their big eyes wide, their heads cocked and ears raised in curiosity, but with bodies tensed and legs crouched to flee. In a moment, they lost nerve and scampered and tumbled away.

I followed at a discrete distance. Naively, they led

me to their den in a tumble of boulders at a place
where ice had worked a crack in the spit and pried it
apart. A pair of shrubby willows had taken root there
and screened the place from the public parking lot
just across the narrow river. The kits vanished into
an opening among the boulders, but they could not
stay hidden for long. Soon they peered out of crevices,
all eyes, and, when they saw that I saw them, ducked
to safety again. We played peek-a-boo.

For a few minutes I enjoyed the game as much as
they, and then I grew uneasy with the fear that my
presence might compromise them. I turned and cir-
cled to the top of the spit to take my leave. But I de-
sired one last glimpse of them. When I looked down,
I saw not the babies, but the mother.

Her hair was sleek and dripping, and she was half-
carrying, half-dragging a lake trout toward the den.
The fish was half again as long as she and thicker in
the body. I could not imagine how she might have
caught it. Mink are fierce and swift, but trout are
equally keen-eyed and wary. Perhaps the trout was
carrion found along the shore or had been released
by the fisherman downriver and had been seized
while it was still disoriented or disabled. It, at any
rate, was quite dead, and the mink was so occupied in
hauling it home that it did not notice me. I watched
until it retreated into the shadow of the willows.

By then dusk had fallen. The air had the graininess
of some black and white photographs, and the lake
looked more like a pool of light than like a body of
water, a dreamy and transfigured landscape in which

floated apparitions of mink and fish, of rock and flower, of birth and death, of day and night, of water and sky. Across the lake the Evening Star appeared, a stab of light in the taut stillness.

Not only with our feet and at our leisure, but also in our dreams, and in the works of our days, we can be saunterers, crusaders in search of whatever may be holy. We know how to undertake this work; it comes to us out of our bones when, wandering an evening away, we suddenly see that all is wild, or when, lying half-awake, as I have been this dreamy morning, we glimpse the wildness in our own hearts.

The squirrel in the tree above me scolds again, and hurls another battery of pine cones down upon my roof. Very well, I mutter, I submit, I submit. I rise, dress, and saunter forth.

PRIME

6 A.M.: *Morning Mists*

I crawl from my tent and stand wide-eyed in the sharp, clean-smelling morning air. Fog shrouds the lake. The island across the way seems to be floating in it. I light my stove and boil a pot of coffee. A chipmunk warily advances to investigate the intrusion. I lean against a rock, drinking in the stillness with the coffee. Suddenly, I feel invisible.

There is the disabling invisibility of being out of place, either in society or in physical space, of not counting, of serving no apparent purpose, of

seeming to be without choices. It is the invisibility
of powerlessness. But that is not the sort of invisibility I feel this morning. I do not feel unnoticed, but
only inconspicuous.

We impose another self-crippling invisibility upon
the world by our habitual inattentiveness, our
somnolence. "Only that day dawns to which we are
awake," Thoreau says. And, "To be awake is to be
alive. I have never yet met a man who was quite
awake. How could I have looked him in the face?"
He thought the best hour of the day was this one,
the first after rising, when we are least asleep and,
therefore, most alive.

The special aliveness of the dawning hour is
nowhere more evident than when you are alone in
some wild place, distant from the distractions of the
workaday morning—the tinkling newspaper, the chattering radio, the scramble to get children dressed and
fed and off to school, to collect yourself for work—
when there is time and silence enough to sit, as I do
now, on a boulder at the edge of the water, listening
to the morning songs of the birds, to the scurry of
critters in the dry litter of the forest, to the splashings
of the traffic entering and leaving the lake.

Every day has its seasons as surely as every year;
there is the springtime of morning, the summer of
midday, the autumn of evening, the winter of night;
and there is the same repeated pattern of wakefulness
and slumber in each—a fresh and even violent energy
in spring, drowsiness after noon, rejuvenation toward
autumnal evening, and finally full-bodied sleep. We

are perhaps more nearly crepuscular—denizens of the dawn and the dusk—than we suppose. An astonishing portion of our lives, at any rate, is spent in outright sleep—two dozen years of an average life—and we pass another year and a half of our waking lives with our eyes closed simply because we have blinked them some 400 million times. How many of our remaining years might we as well have been asleep for all that we failed to notice when we had our eyes nominally open?

As if our natural inclinations toward drowsiness were not sufficient to the day, we have also managed to obscure the world by our feats of engineering. You can, to take one example, traverse the interstate highway system at high speed from coast to coast, through valleys, across plains, over mountains and hills, day merging into night and night into day again, and never encounter an arresting scene, or come into contact with a local culture, or have a conversation that does not hinge upon a commercial transaction, utterly isolated from the land and its people.

The system is a marvel, one of the great public works, heroic in scale, artfully functional, efficient. Perhaps we ought to be proud of it, but what impresses me every time I travel upon it is how extravagantly reductionist it is, how successfully it shrinks to human scale, and to drowsy monotony, even something so vast and various as a continent.

Why climb a mountain when you can achieve a vista just as fine, and more thrilling viscerally, from the observation deck of the nearest skyscraper? Why run a rapids when you can experience the same rush of adrenaline effortlessly and in complete safety at any amusement park? What does any natural bridge offer that the Brooklyn Bridge or the Golden Gate doesn't? Why go to the forest when you can see its marvels a hundred times more vividly on a PBS nature program?

In "The Body and the Earth," the agrarian philosopher Wendell Berry observes that our well-being depends upon the accurate perception that we are small within the scale of the universe. This is something that we have understood—universally, it would seem—until very recently. To know the measure of our smallness is to appreciate our fundamental dependency upon wildness, upon the central alchemy of sun and water and soil that we can neither create, nor replicate, nor dominate. This appreciation saves us, Berry says: from pride, because it teaches us that we can never be gods; and from the despair of destructiveness, because, not tempted to try to be gods, we are also spared the possibility of becoming fiends. We submit ourselves, when we have understood our real place in the universe, to the conditions of our own wildness, which limit our actions and affirm our dependencies.

In acceding to what is vastly larger than ourselves, we are not diminished, but exalted. We assume then our rightful place in the magnificent whole of nature, indistinguishable from it. Grace is the manifestation of a favor from a superior force. The favor we receive in this transaction is life—the possibility, that is, of seeing—and the superior force by which we are endowed with it is the all-seeing Creation: the great wildness at the heart of the universe. We are heirs of the grace of wildness.

To deny this grace, to turn away from the Creation toward our own creations, inevitably diminishes us, as Berry remarks, "because, say what we will, once we build beyond a human scale, once we conceive ourselves as Titans or as gods, we are lost in magnitude; we cannot control or limit what we do. . . . If we have built towering cities, we have raised even higher the cloud of megadeath. If people are as grass before God, they are as nothing before their machines."

Another consequence of living in such a world is the helpless, often foolish, way in which we bow to expertise at every turn, discounting the possibilities— the reality, even—of our own experience. I was driving in a Minnesota blizzard one day, stupidly determined to keep a speaking date. My car was buffeted by a fierce northwesterly wind, my hands tightly clasped the steering wheel, my eyes strained to make out the road, the nerves in my fingertips were on edge, alert to the possibility of a fatal skid into an oncoming truck. In the midst of all this, I risked disaster to turn on the radio. Then I realized why I had done it. I depended upon the radio to certify the reality of the storm that I already knew in every cell of my body.

Years ago, a companion and I were standing in London directly in the shadow of the Tower of Big

Ben, perhaps the best-known clock in the English-speaking world. We had spent the morning doing the tourist rounds, and it seemed as if it ought to be lunchtime. A Londoner approached just as we were considering that possibility. My friend hailed him. "Excuse me, sir," she said, "do you have the time?"

She immediately regretted the words, but it was too late.

The Londoner fixed her in a withering gaze. "You've got to be kidding," he said tartly, and passed on by.

We are so accustomed to receiving the world on outside authority that the possibility of extracting real information from it on our own escapes us. We may live in a time when information is exploding, but the question is whether the explosion is of any use to us. In the practice of our everyday lives, at any rate, we become less competent and more dependent every day. We work for big organizations in which our own roles are always supporting and seldom in-strumental; we dwell in big cities, remote from any relationship with the earth that is not passively con-sumptive; we live encumbered by our conveniences, the workings of which we do not understand, and which we cannot fix when they fail. Once during an extended power outage a friend, who had no heat and no way of cooking, confessed that she couldn't even clean her teeth, since the only instrument she owned for this purpose was electrically powered.

I drain the last drop of coffee from my aluminum cup and return to the stove for a refill. I carry it back down to the lakeshore and sit on a boulder. The sun has almost cleared the tops of the trees. Its first direct rays penetrate the shroud of morning mist overhanging the lake. The island that seemed to be floating in midair has come down to earth again. The mist slowly vaporizes in the heat of the morning sun, palpable now upon the backs of my hands.

In a minute, I will stow my few belongings—they will fit into a single pack with a volume of three thousand cubic inches—and carry them down to the edge of the water. I will right my canoe and launch it, position the pack so that the canoe will track properly, take my paddle, climb aboard, and set out alone, under my own power, bound for a place in the universe that is entirely new to me.

I am not under the delusion that I will set out as a simple child of nature. The canoe I paddle is easy to portage—it weighs only thirty-two pounds—because its core is made of Kevlar. The fibers in my sleeping bag are of Holofil. The jacket that will keep me warm and dry should it rain is made of Gore-Tex. The food in my pack is lightweight and compact because it has been freeze dried. I am tied, even here, by the technologically marvelous strings of human invention.

But I am also, in many ways, set free by this journey, by necessity awakened to the world at hand, and so made more alive to it. If I should become lost, nobody will show me the way home. If a storm should arise, the technological sophistication of my canoe will not save me; by my own wits I will tack against the breaking waves and make my way safely to solid ground. If I should stumble and fall, cracking my ribs against a boulder, there will be nobody to bind up my wounds. No meterologist will forecast the weather; I must read it myself. The thin walls of my tent may keep me dry, but they will shield me from no danger. If I grow bored, no one will entertain me. When I am despondent, I will need to find my own cheer. It is I who will haul the water, and chop the wood, and catch and clean and fry the fish, and make the bed that I will lie down upon when evening comes.

I am freed from my customary slumber because I have made myself vulnerable, and because in my vulnerability I am cast upon my competence, and because, appreciating the limits of my competence, I open my senses. I hear more, see more, taste more, smell more, feel more. The world comes to me like a shock of icy water this foggy wilderness morning. My pores gasp, and the world enters them. I am filled with the world, indistinguishable from it. I feel invisible.

I launch my canoe, enter it, put down my paddle, pull against the water, and slide forward into the unknown.

TIERCE

9 A.M.: *Water, the Canoe, Rock Paintings*

I grew up in tallgrass prairie country. There the sky predominates, the soils are deep and black, the few stones heaved up by the frost are destined to become fencepost ornaments (or were in the days when there

were still fences), and the surface waters run in lan-
guid, silty streams, or collect in shallow, fetid marshes
rimmed with cattails. It is, to most eyes, a forbidding
landscape, ugly, boring, and faintly sinister, like all
unbounded places. But because I knew it long before
I considered any other, I still feel most at home there.
Many landscapes, I suppose, are more beautiful than
mine, but beauty is not everything in a landscape,
any more than it is in a face. So it took me nearly
forty years to venture into the Boundary Waters
Canoe Area, although I am a Minnesotan by birth
and conviction and a traveler in wild places by voca-
tion and compulsion.

The BWCA, as it is locally known, was the
first national forest to be set aside as wilderness.
It remains the largest roadless area east of the
Rocky Mountains in the continental United States.
Extending from Minnesota into Quetico Provincial
Park in Ontario, Canada, this island of wildness en-
compasses five million acres along the Canadian
Shield, where lies exposed some of the Earth's primal
bedrock. It is a land of dense forests and thick bogs, of
rocky ridges and deep, clear lakes, home to moose and
black bears, timber wolves and loons, pine martens
and flying squirrels, lynx and beavers. Its lakes
number in the thousands, closely spaced and inter-
connected, a great lacework sheet of moving water.

Although readily accessible by canoe, it is not
easily navigable. When I venture into it alone, I carry
my compass on a string around my neck. I need to
consult it often, given my disastrously faulty sense of

direction, and I fear losing it. Without the compass,
I would be a danger to myself, commitable to some
institutions. I assumed that this was an individual
failing until I read Calvin Rustrum, a fine, now ne-
glected canoe country writer. "Even most Indians and
white woodsmen, who seem to have an uncanny ability to find their way in their own region," he writes in
North American Canoe Country, "often fare badly
in complex water areas, once they are beyond their
own particular, familiar territory. . . . Considerable
research has gone into the study of man's sense of
direction, and the results have been quite conclusive:
He has no *innate* sense of direction."

There are few signs and trail markers in the canoe
country to point the way, a policy I wish were followed in all of the nation's wilderness preserves. The
possibility of getting lost is among those that define
the wilderness experience. Everyone who has spent
much time in wilderness has been lost at least once,
although few have admitted it, just as few confess the
fear, loneliness, and misery that are equally inherent
in the experience. Being in wilderness is never deliri-
ously, ceaselessly epiphanic. Perhaps more people
who feel inadequate to the test would be encouraged
to try the wild if we who advocate it were more honest about our own blunders and tremblings.

At the same time, most guidebook writers, with
one eye, perhaps, on the liability lawyers, solemnly
sermonize against going into a wilderness alone,
quite correctly pointing out all the horrible mis-
fortunes that might befall you if you do, but never

admitting the incomparable pleasure (and fear, and loneliness, and misery) that they have gained from their own solo travels. Of course one doesn't venture alone into a wilderness stupidly: ill-prepared, inexperienced, inadequately equipped. But if one cares deeply about wilderness, one eventually does go alone, and finds that every subsequent journey, alone or in company, has been enriched by it.

I have twice, while alone, come close to serious harm, perhaps to death, but in neither instance would a companion have prevented the danger, and in one—a fall from a cliff high above treeline, burdened with a fully loaded and securely fastened backpack, into an icy tarn—I could not, I think, have been saved either, except by the bit of luck that got me through: I landed not in the depths of the lake but on a slightly submerged ledge jutting into it, all my bones intact, and did not lose my footing. What I have risked, I have also gained: The silence deep in the wilderness and the one at the center of the human heart are sublime and serene, and they cannot be heard except when alone, and over a broad margin of time and distance. There are some communications, such as those from the stars, that require a greater darkness than can be found at the edges of society.

Canoe country lakes are often small, and it is surprisingly easy to forget how many of them you have crossed in a day of paddling. The most detailed topographical maps are, at best, approximately helpful. Only the biggest of the numerous islands show on

them. In a day's journey you will pass many confus-
ing bays and inlets that look much more substantial
than anything appearing on your maps. And you
travel these lakes seated, or kneeling, in a canoe,
scarcely a yard above the waterline; your angle of vision obscures the whole pattern of even a single small
lake. Unless you, unlike me, are adept at climbing
tall trees or scaling sheer cliffs, there are few vantages
from which to view the landscape at a clarifying distance. Traveling in this country is like making your
way through a vast maze.

A prairie person covets horizons, long views,
openness. The closed and canopied spaces of dense
forests feel, in contrast, confining and vaguely sinister.
The peculiar terror of prairies is that there is no place
to hide; in forests it is that so much is concealed.

The prairie world abounds in light. During much
of the day it is direct and mercilessly harsh; there is
an awful frankness about it, hard to accept, but, in the
end, bracing. A person accustomed to such light finds
the shadowy world of the forest at first subduing, then
funereal, and only after long acquaintance peaceful.

Neither forest nor prairie, actually, much suits
the human eye. We began in the trees, but it was
on the savannas that we first came into our own as
a species. Our lawns and gardens, our cemeteries,
our college campuses, our city parks, our golf
courses: those places where we recreate nature in
idealized form are built on the model, carried by our
ancestors from Africa to Europe and from Europe to
North America, of the savanna: widely spaced trees,

underplanted with short grasses and flowering plants, interspersed with gentle streams or quiet pools of water: places with both long views and discrete edges, where there is both strong light and shade, where land and water converge.

From the perspective of the paddler, the canoe country, although forested, recapitulates the pattern of the savanna: it is a landscape of open spaces bounded by edges that offer hiding places. One landscape feature of nearly universal appeal is the path that curves or moves through a series of constrictions, affording always the prospect of a fresh view just around the bend or beyond the next obstruction. This, too, is an attribute of savannas, and a feature of every satisfying garden. The best gardens organize these changes in prospect to coincide with contrasting patterns of light and shade.

The canoe country is, in this respect, classically compelling. Every lake makes a bright opening in the shadowy forest. The lakes, formed by glacial striations or fault lines, may stretch for miles, narrow and wider in the middle than at either end. Many of them, from the seat of a canoe, appear to curve gently, so that when you launch out upon one, the portage that lies at the far end remains long obscured. When you reach it, you find a narrow trail, a shaded opening in the forest, which usually climbs a ridge, or a succession of them, and descends again to another sunlit sliver of translucent water.

So you are led on, as down a garden path, from light to shade and back again into the light; from open place to narrows or bend, and back into the open; from the clamor of darkness toward the silence of light; from the ambiguity of shadow toward the purity of light; obsessed to discover what lies ahead, just out of sight. One mystery unfolds into the next. The journey is, in the American tradition, the transcendental one, from meanness toward the sublime, from sound toward silence, above all toward the silence of the soul, which is a kind of light, a luminescence, mirrored in the eye, in the sky, in the stillness of waters.

There is a rhythm in the pattern of paddles and portages as hypnotic, once your body is attuned to it, as the beating of drums. Both paddling and portaging are, in themselves, matters of rhythm, the former a rhythm of the upper body, the latter a rhythm of the feet, both of ancient origin, the rhythms of the drumbeats on the long-ago savannas. They are wonderfully complementary. After a few days of breaking in, it is possible to sustain either without great strain from dawn until dusk. You have achieved, when this happens, a kind of bodily fluency, an incarnation of grace.

The canoe itself is such an incarnation, one of the inspired human designs, elegant, efficient, simple, adaptable, perfectly fitted to its purpose. It is sleek enough to slip through the water, even when it bears heavy loads; stable in turbulence; capable of tracking a straight line in a wind, but maneuverable through a rapids; light enough to be carried, but tough enough to withstand collisions and scrapes; stealthy in an environment where silence rules and every sound

carries enormous distances; and it can be built—
although it seldom is anymore—from materials abun-
dantly at hand locally. It is a tool supremely suited
to its place, a work of indigenous genius.

I set out this morning intent upon making my
passage from one lake to the next by way of a narrow, slow-moving river. The route will carry me to a
widening of it where there are rock paintings, one
minor site among scores of them in this country.
I want to see the paintings because, obscure though
the intentions now are of the people who created
them, who are also unknown, I hope that they
might tell me something about what it means to
be indigenous.

To be inherent to the place: this is a feeling that,
despite our long habitation here, we Americans have
yet fully to experience. Our presence on this continent still seems somehow tentative, our roots still
underdeveloped, our claim to ownership still fraught
with moral doubt. "Our day of dependence, our long
apprenticeship to the learning of other lands, draws
to a close. The millions that around us are rushing
into life, cannot always be fed on the sere remains
of foreign harvests," Ralph Waldo Emerson boldly
declared in 1837, electrifying his Harvard audience.
But more than a century and a half since, we still
perceive that ours remains a Western rather than
an American culture, and when we speak of *native*
Americans, it is not the founders of our republic or
their descendants to whom we refer, but an older race

of discoverers, who probably followed the ice south from Siberia. "We may have colonized this continent," the geneticist Wes Jackson says, "but we have not yet discovered it."

My own voyage of discovery carries me this morning across the shallows of the lake over bottom boulders that look so near in the refracted light of the crystalline waters and so mysteriously alive in the ripples of my wake that I think they might at any moment rise up and seize me. If anything can claim to possess this place surely it is they, who have lain here for centuries, receptive to the great turnings of the seasons, in times of ice and thaw, of pollen and ash. I wish for them the power of speech, that they might tell me what I am in search of, for I do not know whether it is myself I seek, or the land, or the connection between them, or if, in fact, there is any difference.

At the narrows of the lake I cross over a little arch of land and put in at the river, which, in this shadowy morning light, looks like a dark artery, or vein, running deep in the dense body of a forest so tropically profuse that it seems impervious, foreign, organismic, a place where the trees cannot be seen for the forest. I stifle my breath, so raucous it seems in the surrounding stillness, and paddle my way dreamily upriver, turning the blade at the end of each stroke and pulling it forward underwater so as not to violate the reverential air.

Around one bend I pass a huge beaver lodge;

around the next, a reedy marsh in which a bull moose, magnificently racked, feeds without interruption, as if I were merely a bit of flotsam; and around the next, a pileated woodpecker, which takes precipitously to the air, its scarlet crest glowing in a shaft of sunlight, crying what sounds a curse. The cry echoes back, and the forest falls silent again.

Faintly at first, like a whisper of wind, I hear the sound of running water. As I approach it, its language becomes more distinct, the babble of many voices in an unfamiliar language. And then I am upon the rapids, the water slipping over stones like liquid silk, its voice now a low murmur, the sound of an astonished crowd.

I portage around the falls, a distance of a few rods, and when I arrive at its upper end and am about to take to the river again, I see a flash of yellow in the shallows beside the canoe. A clump of irises blooms there. I know from their goldenness, the indigenous irises being blue, that they, like me, have traveled far to reach this place. They are fleur-de-lis, specimens of which were carried by traders on the Silk Route from Asia to Europe, becoming there the ensign of the kings of France, and from Europe to North America by French fur traders, who thought them a touch of home—the sort of confusion that perhaps all vagabond humans share. Once when I was a newspaper editor, I sent a young journalist to interview the poet John Berryman on the occasion of some new prize, and when she asked him about his roots, a phrase then in currency, he exploded. "Roots!" he bellowed. "What do you think I am, some goddamn *plant?*"

Thoreau, reading Gray's *Manual of Botany*, was inspired to think how nearly like plants we in fact are, if we are healthy, especially in the matter of roots. "The mind is not well balanced and firmly planted, like the oak," he wrote in his journal, "which has not as much root as branch, whose roots like those of the white pine are slight and near the surface. One half of the mind's development must still be root,—in the embryonic state, in the womb of nature, more unborn than at first. For each successive new idea or bud, a new rootlet in the earth. The growing man penetrates yet deeper by his roots into the womb of things. The infant is comparatively near the surface, just covered from the light; but the man sends down a taproot to the center of things."

This is not, by and large, the country of oaks. Here the shallow-rooted white pines reign, or used to before the days of the lumbermen, and in any case, given the shallowness of the soil and the impenetrability of the bedrock that lies just beneath it, deep taproots are not generally an option. I see, however, how firmly the balsam that lies uprooted just upriver has embraced that rock, raising a massive chunk of it as it fell, even though it had not been grounded in the darkest regions of the Earth.

And I see how successfully, how gracefully these Asiatic irises have taken hold here at an ancient crossroads of the global village, not one of the

highways traveled by the birds or the winds, but a
lane opened by the wanderlust of enterprising humans. If the fleur-de-lis are not by now indigenous
here, if they will always be, as the botanists say, alien,
still they look securely at home.

They remind me that although we think of this
place now as wilderness, as a refuge where nature
might make a last defense against the ravages of culture, and although it is a forbidding place in which to
make a living, nevertheless it has been occupied by
humans for at least eight or nine thousand years. It is
likely that the portage I have just crossed was already
in more or less continuous use before the first artifact
of my own civilization was struck. The ancient cross-
ings may sometimes now be obscured, Sigurd Olson,
the bard laureate of this country, has written in *The
Singing Wilderness*, but "they are always there, and
when you pack your outfit across them you are part
of a great company that has passed before. . . . The
way of a canoe is the way of the wilderness and of a
freedom almost forgotten. It is an antidote to insecu-
rity, the open doorway to waterways of ages past and
a way of life with profound and abiding satisfactions.
When a man is part of his canoe, he is part of all that
canoes have ever known."

I paddle again upriver until I round another bend
and come upon the widening of it that I have sought.
Along one bank, an ice-polished face of granite rises,
perhaps three hundred yards long and fifty feet high.
When I draw near to it, I see that it slopes toward me

and find myself enshrouded in its perpetual shadow. The rock is dark, stained, and rifled with cracks, but unsullied by lichens, and when I draw very close, I can see a long line of markings, just above the level of my eyes, the color of old blood, but faded, some beyond recognition.

I paddle to the head of the cliff and drift past the paintings, turn and do it again, and again. A few of the markings are immediately recognizable: a canoe, a moose, a human figure, a thunderbird. Others, including the most prominent figure here, which looks to me like the backside of a mission-style rocking chair, are utterly mysterious. The markings were, it is thought, applied with pigments made from animal grease, or the eggs of gulls, or the roe of fish, and tinctures of iron-bearing oxides, probably, judging from their durability, by people who lived here within the last two thousand years. One or two of them, in a rudimentary way, are even readable. The thunderbird, for example, was a supernatural creature living high in the heavens which bellowed and flashed its presence by flapping its wings to make thunder and by blinking its eyes to produce lightning.

Beyond these few facts little is known. It is not clear why they were made; or why they were made *where* they were made; or what, in general, they signify; or to whom they were addressed. This much seems clear: that they were messages; and this much more can be conjectured: that not all of the messages were addressed to humans, that some of them, at least, were meant to be—perhaps still are— communications with the gods, who were once thought to dwell in this land, and perhaps still do.

These people, whoever they were, were not indigenous. They also came from somewhere else— they may even have come from the home-place of the fleur-de-lis—and followed the glaciers of the last Ice Age northward as they melted, and settled here, and came to know the place spiritually as much as physically. When the Europeans arrived, these forecomers were the natives, and so they remain. It may be that this is what it means to be native to a place: to know it intimately enough so that one can say where lives its spirit, or spirits.

"Whatever their interpretation," Sigurd Olson writes of the painted rocks in *Listening Point*, "they marked the period during which Stone Age man emerged from the dark abyss of his past into the world of mind and soul." Olson was not indigenous to this place either, but he stayed long enough, once he had arrived, to notice, to take account of—to discover—and so at last to learn to sing its poetry. Let us also agree that this was sufficient to have made him native.

INTERSTICES

The Economy of the Canoe Country

The busiest route into the heart of Quetico Provincial Park, the part of this wilderness north of the United

States border with Canada, begins on Moose Lake
and is made by way of Prairie Portage, where there is
now a Canadian customs office. It was once a resting
place of the voyageurs. Motorized boats are allowed
that far, although from the boat landing on Moose
Lake northward, the country is all now unsettled and
preserved as wilderness. In recent years, many—
perhaps a majority—of the canoeists crossing the
border by this route have taken advantage of tow services to be sped into the heart of the wilderness. The
canoeist who paddles the whole way—to do so adds
only half a day to the journey, coming and going—
is assaulted at the peak of the summer season by a
relentless parade of power boats, burdened to the
gunwales with canoes and supplies, their engines
revved to full speed, their whine shattering the silence of what is nominally a wilderness preserve,
their fat wakes washing steadily against what might
otherwise be peaceful shores.

To travel in this way is the wilderness equivalent
of journeying overland by jet aircraft rather than meandering the back roads from one city to another. It
is to cast away all the rich ceremony of arrival in the
wilderness and of departure from it, which is, after
all, central to the possibility that a journey will be
refreshing: the sense of having come a long way, of
contrast between what is familiar and what has been
newly experienced. Such sensations, to be fully
realized, need to be savored, to unfold slowly, in all
of their detail. It is the difference between fast food
gulped down on the run and a meal lovingly prepared

and lingered over with friends. When I am being tossed in the wake of one of these ferries, I am angry that my own efforts to approach the wilderness reverently have been so rudely violated. Later, I am sorry for all that those who have sped past have sacrificed of the real journey for a few hours and a few miles of convenience.

No engine yet devised can speed the workings of the spirit. If you have hurried to get into the wilderness physically, still you will not be there mentally or emotionally. You will still need to decompress; to set aside the cares and preoccupations of the world you have just left; to slow yourself down to canoe time; to release yourself from the dictates of the clock and to submit to the ancient cycles of sunrise and sunset; to allow your sensory organs to open wide again—the overstimulation of the industrial world of our everyday lives causes our bodies, in sympathy for themselves, to damper down. Hurtling into the wilderness under engine power saves no time at all if it is the experience of the wilderness you are after; it may, in fact, waste time.

Perhaps human beings in every age have labored under some characteristic insensibility. The distinguishing handicap of our own age is our weakness for false economies. We love every kind of efficiency, so long as it is spendthrift. Our agricultural economy is the paradigm. We have, over the past half century, driven all but a handful of our farmers from the land, at an enormous expense of soil, water, fuel, and biological diversity. At the same time, we have accepted the unemployment and underemployment of millions of our citizens as reasonable and normal. If this is efficient—as is widely claimed—then the logical question—which Wendell Berry has raised—is, What are people *for?*

By the same token, if the wilderness needs to be approached at mechanized speed, with every possible convenience of home in tow, then what is *wilderness* for? Why not simply stay at home? I have encountered people who carried alarm clocks into the wilderness!

We have the benefit of, but have never mastered, the instruction of Thoreau. If he has walked to the next town while his neighbor has taken the train, Thoreau asks, which of them has saved time? The cost of a train ticket is a day's labor, he says, but it takes him only a day to walk there, so he will already have arrived before his neighbor has set out, having earned, along the way, all the benefits of a day of walking in the countryside. Which of us, he asks, has practiced the greater economy?

As it happens, the economics of the canoe country compute in exactly the same way. It costs half a day's wages to be ferried to the Quetico border. I can paddle there just as quickly. In doing so, I will have earned not only the pleasures of the journey, which were my objective in going, but also the benefits of half a day's preparation for the experience of being in the wilderness, which I will have needed in any case, and I get to keep the half-day's wages besides. But we have lost our capacity for rational economics; the ferry boats do a brisk business.

We have lost our economic bearings largely because we have come to a narrow and debilitating sense of what it means to be efficient. "Performing or functioning in the best possible manner with the least waste of time and effort," my dictionary says. Time and effort are measures of labor; we now understand efficiency to be chiefly a matter of saving labor. This makes sense only in an industrial economy, and then only if the worth of what we do can be quantified in dollars and cents.

But not every economy worth nurturing is industrial. The economy of nature is, by industrial standards, hopelessly profligate. Industrialism values uniformity, reliability, predictability. Manufacturing the greatest number of things in the least amount of time with the least possible investment of human energy depends upon the greatest possible degree of conformity.

The great British biologist J. B. S. Haldane, asked for his conception of God, in whom he did not believe, is said to have replied, "He is inordinately fond of beetles." If an industrialist had been in charge of designing nature, he would never have imagined anything so preposterous as beetles. There are perhaps a million and a half species of them on Earth—some 350,000 of them have already been named—as compared with about five thousand species of mammals, in what we presume to be the

Age of Mammals. It was by counting the variety of beetles to be found in the crowns of a certain species of tree in the Panamanian rainforest—some twelve hundred species were collected from nineteen trees over a period of three years—that we were suddenly obliged, as recently as 1982, to revise upward by a factor of fifteen our estimation of the number of species currently alive on the planet.

The beetles have in common a moderate size and, as compared with the other insects, a seemingly modest adaptation in form: a pair of anterior wings that function not for flight but as protective covers for the posterior wings. Had an industrialist been put in charge of designing a natural world efficient by contemporary standards, he would not have thought this variation on the idea of the insect desirable in the first place, but supposing he had, he certainly would not have regarded a million and a half variations on the variation as necessary or useful. In the industrial sense of efficiency, fewer kinds of beetles—if there needed to be beetles at all—could surely have been made to suffice. Indeed, even in an ecological sense, it is not at all clear that so many kinds of beetles serve any vital purpose. And then to devise them in every color of the rainbow! To endow them with fecundity as a strategy for surviving extravagant mortality! To expend so much design attention on something with such a short life span! (It is true, of course, that beetles have survived pretty much in their present form for a hundred million years, and that they probably have a better chance of enduring environmental holocaust than most other creatures, but the industrialist's eye is not on the long run.)

Before the current century, the emphasis of meaning in the word "efficiency" was not on productivity, but on adequacy. The compact edition of the *Oxford English Dictionary*, reflecting its age, defines efficiency as "fitness or power to accomplish, or success in accomplishing, the purpose intended; adequate power, effectiveness, efficacy." By this definition, a canoe is an entirely efficient craft for the exploration of the Quetico-Superior country, even though it is slower and requires more physical labor than a motor boat: it is adequately powerful, it is effective, and it is, especially, efficacious: it is, that is, an appropriate means to the end, assuming that one travels into Quetico-Superior country to encounter the country itself, and to measure oneself against it. In either case, both speed and artificial power are disadvantages; they are, by the classical definition, in fact, inefficiencies.

Profit—the end product of efficiency—has undergone a similar evolution in meaning. When efficiency meant an adequate power appropriately applied to a desirable end, profit referred to anything useful. Both a loaf of bread and a day of leisure could once have been said, with exactly the same meaning, to be profitable. Now, when we think of efficiency as a savings of time and effort, we define profit as a pecuniary gain. The effect of this shift in meanings is to divorce the idea of profit from the attribute of usefulness, which is its essential quality.

This divorce has narrowed and cheapened our sense of work: it counts as profitless every labor undertaken for some cause other than economic gain; but more importantly, it has cheapened our sense of ourselves: if we count as profitable even work that is of no use, and if we count as loss every labor undertaken solely out of love—if we deny ourselves the possibilities of life as an unfolding of gifts—then we cheat ourselves out of every kind of luxury.

Instead of approaching a journey as if each part of it had some unexpected gift to offer, as if it were an experience to be savored, to be allowed to unfold in its own way and in its own time, we count minutes and labors as if they were pennies to be pinched, saving an hour here and an exertion there, and find, when we have arrived, that we have never left home at all.

The efficiencies of the canoe country are all of the prodigal kind, and none of the profits are pecuniary. If we would experience it, we must learn again to wager in an older and wiser economy.

SEXT

Noon: Rock, the Swim, the Dragonfly

It is noon, and I have sought respite on a knoll of granite, in which the etchings of the glaciers of ten thousand years ago are still vivid, out of considerations as various and complex, as amalgamated, as the materials in the rock. I have been paddling since early morning. The muscles in my arms are weary; my legs, which I have alternately stretched and tucked under the seat of my canoe, are cramped; and I am hungry. I have passed through early mists down the winding Kawishiwi River, have glided so stealthily past a bull moose feeding on water plants in a marsh that I did not disturb its breakfast, have examined the residences of beavers, have admired the bloom of irises, have savored the melody of a white-crowned sparrow, have made the acquaintance of a loon so near that I could peer into the startling scarlet of its eye, have threaded a bewildering maze of islands and ventured across open water in the dazzling glare of the high morning sun: I stop out of consideration for all that has transpired, that I might lock it in memory. I stop because it is the middle of the day: out of consideration for habit. I stop because I have traveled for a long time on the thin skin of lakes and rivers, an alien place: out of consideration for my standing as a creature of the earth. I stop because when this small island appeared on the horizon, it beckoned to me: to honor my curiosity.

As I approach the island, I see that it is a walled fortress, presenting only a narrow, pebbled slit upon which to land. I coast toward it and backpaddle until, parallel to the beach, I have drifted smoothly to shore. This manuever pleases me, as does the proper use of any tool. I step onto the beach, remove my pack, and lift the canoe from the water. For a moment I am disoriented; my inner ears need to adjust to the sudden equilibirium of solid ground. Overhead, herring gulls cry, as they do in ports everywhere. I feel as much the mariner as Captain Ahab.

Now that I am ashore, I can sense, as I could not while I was still paddling, the elixir of tiredness in my body, a pacific contentment, in part induced by pheromones released during exertion, the natural drugs, also set loose when we laugh, that make physical labor so addictive, so satisfying.

I climb with my pack to the top of the island and find there a shaded, grassy opening in a clump of birches. The shade feels cool and soothing. I realize that my skin has been burning in the intense light reflected from the water. My skin is gritty with the salts of dried sweat. When I lift my eyelids, they feel like fine sandpaper.

I sit on the grass—so luxuriant a patch of it is rare in this country—and eat my lunch of dried fruit and nuts, cheese and sausage, and a bar of chocolate, washing it down with long draughts of water drawn from the lake, soft as rain. The island seems the more remote because my repast is undisturbed by the opportunists—the chipmunks and gray jays— that hang around more frequented campsites.

The lines of communication here about food free for the scavenging are sometimes stupendously effective. One night, when I had filleted a bass for supper, I took its remains down to the lakeshore and laid them on a rock for the gulls, though I had not seen one all day. Within minutes, the place was as rowdy as a rock concert. Half a dozen herring gulls had converged out of nowhere and had begun to fight and scream, in their surpassingly disagreeable way, over the few scraps of fish. At first, the smallest of them

had possession of the prize piece—the head—too large
to swallow, which it neverthless valiantly defended
against the shrieks and dive-bombings of its larger
fellows, until the assaults became merciless, and it
dropped the head and retreated, ignoring the lesser
but ingestible scraps of fish floating nearby. The same
fracas repeated itself half a dozen times. Finally one
of the biggest gulls managed to lift into the air with
the head of the bass clamped in its bill and flapped off
to the next lake, hotly pursued by its taunting, but
weaker, mates.

I could not imagine how the gulls had found my
few scraps so swiftly, except that they had obviously
been biding their time somewhere nearby in the hope
of just such an opportunity. It left me a bit unnerved
that they had. All the rest of the evening, I felt un-
comfortably conspicuous, keenly aware that although
I was, so far as I knew, the solitary human in the
neighborhood, I was a long way from being alone.
I tried to avoid imagining how many pairs of eyes
and ears were tracking my every move.

After the meal, I clamber back down to the cove
where I landed my canoe, strip, and plunge into
the lake, so deep a few feet out that it looks almost
green. Although I expect its coldness, it arrives, as it
does every time, with a shock. My heart leaps, skips
a beat, and I gasp. I thrash about, noisy as a moose,
duck my head a few times to rinse the grime from
my hair, and turn up on my back. Because I spent
my boyhood far from any swimming hole, my
technique has never advanced much beyond the

dog paddle. I retain a landlubber's fear of water. I
have learned enough about it to believe that if I don't
fight it—if, my women friends say, I give up the male
delusion of being in control—I will float, but I have
learned little enough so that every time I try, I think
myself the beneficiary of a small miracle. The sun is
bright and the season advanced; there is a thin zone
of tolerably warm water near the lake's surface. I
float in it as long as I dare, take one last headlong
dive, reveling in the balming coolness of the lake
against my sunburned face, and crawl up the algae-
slickened boulders to shore. A bath towel is one of
the encumbrances I forego on these trips; I shake
myself and sit in the sunlight, like an animal, to dry.

While I am basking in the pleasure of the two
baths, the one in the water, and the one in the sun,
feeling as unfettered in my nakedness as a dog off the
leash, the corner of my eye catches a miniscule com-
motion. The ice of centuries has wedged a crack
in the ledge of granite that I am sitting on. When I
look closely, I see along its edge a creature as green
as a fresh pea—at first I mistake it for a luna moth—
emerging from the ferocious-looking carapace of a
water insect.

The carapace is the nymphal form of one of the
Macromiidae, an order of dragonflies. It is an inch
and a half long, has very long legs, which grip the
stone tightly, like the fingers of a baby, and a squat,
chitinous abdomen, a bit larger than my thumbnail,
barbed at the edges of the plates, that resembles the
shell of a turtle. Its oval head is preposterously small

for its body and disproportionately apportioned to a pair of dark eyes. Between them, there are two antennae, and, between the antennae, a prominent horn with a nasty hook. The nymph is a dark gray-brown, the dreary color of the silts at the bottom of the lake, where it has spent its sedentary life for the past year or two, preying promiscuously on practically everything that has passed—other nymphs, mosquito larvae, water bugs, even small fish—by means of a long, double-hinged exterior lip, tucked under the thorax when it is not in use, so big as partially to obscure the creature's face. This lip is equipped with a pair of sharp, moveable hooks. The prey approaches. The dragonfly nymph skewers it on the thorns of its suddenly ejaculated tongue, able then to snack on it at its leisure, employing for the purpose a powerful pair of mandibles. It breathes through its ass.

As I watch, the fierce, ugly creature's body splits down its back at the mid-dorsal line and from it, in incredibly slow motion, emerges an enormous adult dragonfly. First the thorax appears, then the head with eyes so huge they nearly meet at center brow, then the six long legs, which grope for footing on the rock, and finally the long abdomen, soft and crumpled as a freshly washed swatch of cotton. The whole creature is five or six inches long, dwarfing the skin of its nymphal self. It is as ridiculous as a crowd of clowns emerging from a toy car.

The limp creature dangles impassively for a moment, and then draws in a big gulp of air, leaving behind forever the gills of its water existence, committing itself to a new life on the wing. Its abdomen suddenly stiffens, and, with a faint shivering, its double wings begin to unfurl and straighten. They look soft, wet, and silken. Blood has begun to course through the dragonfly's veins. The creature is perpendicular to the rock, its forward pair of legs hooked over the top of the boulder, its head aiming toward the Milky Way.

For more than an hour, the creature hangs there, moisture falling a drop at a time from its abdomen, while its wings harden and become translucent and the green of its exoskeleton dulls and becomes etched with a delicate tracery of brown lines, like porcelain cracking with age. I watch it anxiously, knowing that this is its most perilous hour. Immobile, it is ripe for the voracious eyes of any bird, and even something so capricious as a sudden strong breeze might rumple a wing and cripple it for life.

Since it first pulled its abdomen from its nymphal skin, the dragonfly has not moved. Now in a single graceful and seemingly effortless motion it lifts from the rock and takes to the air, which it will scarcely leave until it is finally felled by the first hard freeze of autumn; its long subaqueous respite has passed; it has been born again into a brief moment of exuberant beauty. The transformation is as astonishing, Edwin Way Teale wrote, "as though a trout should suddenly shed its skin and become a robin."

The carapace of the nymph from which the dragonfly emerged still clings to the rock. I reach for it. It has the rock in a death-grip and must be gently pried loose. In my hand, it seems to weigh less than a feather. Were it any less substantial, it would not exist.

I rise and head up the knoll to gather my things. It is time to push on. I suddenly notice the discarded skins of dragonfly nymphs everywhere. I have, it seems, tarried in a paradise of metamorphosis. As I take to the water again, I feel a new man myself.

NONES

3 P.M.: *Wind, Portage Trails, the Storm*

It is the fifth hour of the day, three P.M. A stiff wind is blowing, as it often does at this hour. I am headed into it, as, it seems, I eternally am. I shift my pack toward the bow and move forward myself, onto my knees, to counter the force of the wind, which would otherwise swing me back in the direction from which I have just come.

Once years ago I was marooned for hours in a wind like this. I had set out alone, inexperienced, in a clumsy canoe, intent on catching a mess of crappies around the leeward point of a large island. I was staying on the mainland opposite it. A storm was brewing, and my stringer soon was full. I pulled it in and headed home. But when I rounded the bend toward the cabin, the wind spun me around and sent me back toward the fishing grounds. I tried again, with the same result. I positioned myself in as many ways as I could imagine, but every time I tried to cross the channel from the island to the mainland, my canoe pirouetted.

Although I didn't want to paddle the whole way around the island, there seemed no alternative. When I had arrived at the channel from the opposite side of the island, however, I faced the same problem. I could get to within sight of the cabin, but no matter what I did, I could not hold the canoe in the wind. Around and around I spun, tossing in the waves like a bobber. I cursed. I redoubled my efforts at paddling. I went at the barrier of the wind like a chicken trying to break a fence, over and over, stupidly, blindly, until I was a gibbering mess. In the end, I had to wait out the wind in the shelter of the island. For a long time afterward, I couldn't imagine what anybody saw in canoeing.

Now I expect the wind and welcome it. It is a regularity of the day, like the mists of morning and the mirrored waters of evening, one of the pulses at the heart of the land by which I know it to be well. When I fall to my knees before the wind and dig in hard with the blade of my paddle, I know that before another lake or two has passed, it will be time to put ashore and make a camp for the night.

In becalmed waters, the canoe seems hardly to move. Now, when I struggle just to hold position against the wind in the tricky air currents off the points of the lake, I feel airborne. Our perceptions of nature, I think, are often contrary and misleading in this way, accustomed as we are to falsely imagining ourselves as at the center of things.

I like the moist wind in my face. I like the tiny wake that rises as the canoe cuts through the waves. I like the gentle rocking of the boat. I like the feel of my muscles straining to maintain a forward momentum. I like the way the drops of water falling out of the curls of the combers glisten in the sunlight. I like the sound of wind and water in my ears.

When the wind blows, the whole landscape seems in motion, throbbing with energy. It seems possible that it might, at any moment, explode into something even grander. This watery world is never more exuberantly alive than when it roils in the wind.

Overhead the clouds pass like great ships, stately and powerful. They are dark with rain. They gather and stream forward until they blot out the sun. The light, which has been harsh and white, turns a soft, incandescent yellow. I race for the portage ahead.

I carry the canoe up a forested ridge, brushing against ferns and brackens, stumbling over rocks in the premature twilight. At the other end of the portage, a tiny lake perches on a glacial shelf rimmed with birches. Water lilies, yellow with blossom, float in its rippled shallows, their pads curling in the wind. I double back for the pack. A stream tumbles from the smaller lake into the bigger one, cutting inexorably away at the rock straining to contain it. Here, even the rock is on the move.

There is a sudden stillness, then a gust of wind moaning in the limbs of the trees, then stillness again, and, as I arrive back at the place where I have stashed the canoe, the first patter of raindrops. They are huge and heavy. I see them collide against the surface of the lake, bounce, and fall back again into the saucers they have made. The surface of the lake is covered with tiny concentric rings, as if it were a pot about to boil.

I put my rain jacket on, tuck my pack beneath the overturned canoe, and take shelter in a clump of cedars. The rain quickens, falls nearly in sheets. Its din is deafening. The water beads and runs in tiny rivers down my sleeves. I feel my wrists moistening and the water running down my face and neck. When I can no longer see through the lenses of my glasses, I remove them and tuck them into a pocket. The world becomes a vague blur of wet, writhing blues and greens and grays such as Monet, in the end, saw in his garden.

In twenty minutes, the sky brightens. A minute later, the sun falls, like a spotlight, on the lake dimpled with raindrops. A minute or two after, the rain stops altogether. Overhead, there is blue sky, but in the forest the water continues to drip.

I retrieve my glasses, remove my rain coat, right the canoe and launch it, load the pack, get in myself, and set out across the lake. I am no longer on my knees. The trunks of the birches look as white as snow, the shining rocks as red as blood, and every green leaf glistens like jade. I am in motion again, skimming double-time across the water, inhaling the sweet smell of ozone, intoxicated by the newness of everything.

VESPERS

Evening: Calm Waters, Sunset Rituals

At the height of the summer season in canoe country, it is advisable to begin looking for a place to camp by early afternoon. The best places are quickly taken, and camping is allowed only at designated sites. These are usually situated above the sloping slabs of granite or gneiss that the glaciers cut long ago. They provide convenient landing places for canoes; make natural openings in the forests that, elsewhere, over-shadow the edges of the lakes, unless the shores are lined with cliffs; and offer comfortable prospects upon which to idle, after the evening meal is finished, with a cup of coffee and—if you are a traditionalist— a cigar or pipe, watching the sun fall.

Assisting the sun on its daily journey over the western horizon is one of the necessary labors of any journey into a wilderness. The work requires close attention. If you are with a companion, the conver-sation must be hushed and never too urgent. It will not do to argue or joke the sun away. Patience is a virtue diligently to be practiced at all times, but es-pecially at evening; the sun will not be hurried. It is reticent about crossing the horizon. When it reaches that threshhold, it takes the pause that every drama-tist knows well, the brief sigh of silence, before it makes its exit and the curtain falls. Then, especially, one must not break the mood with unseemly chat-ter or busyness of any kind.

The hours immediately preceding the departure of

the sun are the ones, in the wilderness day, of domesticity. A certain ritual attends them. The canoe, once
landed, must be unloaded and the canoe itself carried
to safe ground and overturned, in case a wind should
rise or rain should fall in the night.

Then one's camp shoes must be located and ex-
changed for one's canoeing shoes, which will have
grown damp and cold during the day's travels. I carry
a pair of high-topped L. L. Bean canvas shoes with
rubber soles, once tan, but now weathered to a comely
gray, like favorite pieces of patio furniture. They are
duplicates of my canoe shoes, but dry. A pair of dry
and familiar shoes, which carry somewhere in their
scuffed, stained, and softened threads the memory of
all the campsites past, are the essential first step in
making of a stopping place a home, however temporary. When they have been donned and securely tied,
and one's toes have found their proper places among
the subtle indentations of the soles, the wet shoes
and socks must be laid out to dry.

Next, the site for the tent—although it will be
obvious, having already been chosen by a thousand
previous occupants—must be carefully scrutinized,
with an eye toward the exact square of maximum
levelness, taking into account the direction in which
runoff waters might flow in the event of a storm, and
how the doorway of the tent must be placed to take
advantage of the first rays of the morning sun. No
matter how many times the spot has been previously
prepared, one must remove, if only ritually, a stray
pebble or two, a bit of twig, and a pine cone, lest one's

slumbers be offended by too casual an approach to the pitching of the tent. Then the ground cloth must be laid, and repositioned, and the tent unfolded upon it, and staked, and raised.

Every wilderness traveler develops a fondness for a reliable tent. It becomes, with frequent use, an island of security, a counterbalance to the sometimes overwhelming instability of travel. Mine is a two-person Eureka Timberline. I bought it many years ago, before I became a solo traveler in wild places, on a whim. It was on sale, and I had the vague notion that I might use it sometime. It was, it turned out, not a whim, but an inspiration: lightweight, easy to pitch without assistance, absolutely dependable. And it was an inducement. Once I owned it, I felt obligated, as a practicing Lutheran, to use it.

My tent has traveled with me thousands of miles since in every kind of terrain and weather. I have been lonely in it, tired and depressed, exhilarated, terrified, contented. I have repaired to it when I was lost, and when I was delighted to have found my way. I have sometimes known, when I retired to it, what my journeyings were about, and sometimes I have been confused and perplexed. Now, whenever I crawl into it, I have the sense of being accompanied. I am reminded of all the places we have been together, all the nights and moods and circumstances we have shared. It seems to me that it, like my camp shoes, in some mystical way carries the memory of those times within its fibers. Portable though it may be, it is, for me, a kind of home.

Where I grew up, in the countryside of western Minnesota, people had home-places. The home-place was where your grandparents lived, perhaps where they had been born, where one of your own parents had been raised, where your father still worked the land. It was the epicenter of familial life, recognized as such not only by you, but also by your friends and neighbors. If you said to a friend, "We're having a picnic Sunday night at the home-place," your friend knew where to go, even though you yourself didn't live there anymore. The home-place was the settling place, the one your forbearers had come to from the old country; the place where, for better or worse, they had concluded to try their fortunes; or it was the final stop in the family's wanderings, the place where luck, or money, or resolve had run out, where one made a last stand.

I was born in the baby boom of the late 1940s, in the year that 2,4-D, the first miracle chemical of industrial agriculture, was introduced. Although farm children had already for generations been forsaking the farm for the brighter opportunities of cities, and although a million farm families were driven by economic forces from the land during my elementary school years, still it was hoped that I, like those of my lineage, would settle down, make my life where I had been born, and someday take over management of the home-place. The idea had its attractions, and I might have been persuaded by them—although I doubt happily—if it had not become obvious by my teens that I was hopelessly ungifted mechanically, and not very adept, either, at concentrating on the details of the farm work at hand.

My mind wandered even when my feet couldn't. I was always catching the drag in the fence at the end of the field and pulling it down, or running out of gas at the wrong end of the farm, or cultivating out the corn rather than the weeds, or letting the grain wagon spill over. My father, in the end, acknowledged that I had better think of something else to do with my life, but he could not accept the idea in his heart. On the day when I left for college, he made it a point not to be around to say goodbye.

I have come to terms with my father's disappointment. I'm quite certain I would have starved had I tried to be a farmer. Still, I often wonder what I left behind when I set out for Minneapolis on that September day so many years ago, my worldly possessions in a cardboard box and a hand-me-down suitcase, throbbing with excitement, but my sense of where I belonged yet in limbo. I think that what I left behind was not farming; not, certainly, the community of which it was a part, about which I then had much less positive feelings than I do now; not family, for my family, like most modern ones, quickly scattered to distant cities; not even the place itself, for place is, as Robert Farrar Capon says, not a location, but a session; what matters most about it is not where you are but who, or what, you are with; it becomes real only in the engagement between the two. What I had left behind was the home-place.

I have lived and visited since in many places.

Some of them I have lingered in, or visited frequently, long enough or often enough for familiarity. They are places, even, that I have come to depend upon, that give my life shape and dimension, in the sense, at least, that they are in some way measures of myself. When I return to a book I have often read, or to a piece of music long familiar, or to the liturgies I have recited almost since I was an infant, or when I visit an old friend after a long absence, I find in the stirrings of my heart, in the memories that are provoked, in the dreams that follow, a gauge of the ways in which I have changed, or stayed the same.

"My, how big you've gotten!" the out-of-town aunts would invariably exclaim when we gathered for a baptism or graduation, a wedding or funeral. I was always, in the way of children, exasperated at their stupidity. What did they think, that I was going to remain forever two? I knew that I had been accepted as an adult when they started to say, "Well, you haven't changed a bit!" "It would turn your hair blue to know the ways," I would think. And then I was suddenly old enough to be flattered, and before long I found myself saying the same things to the children of friends.

When we were preschoolers, my sister and I often wandered down the lane to the neighbors on the next farm, a kindly and elderly couple who talked to us seriously and kept a bowl of caramels, and had a refrigerator, a device as exotic to us as a Martian spaceship, in which there was ice cream. They liked us and we adored them. Then I moved to Minneapolis,

and to other places, and my parents died, and for
a long time I put them and the home-place out of
mind.

One night I was invited back there to tell about
a book I had written. With some misgivings, I went.
Irene, the woman on the next farm, had died, I
learned. Indeed, she had been buried that very afternoon. But Jake came to the talk, a gift that both over-
welmed and shamed me. How selfish and neglectful
I have been, I thought. I hugged him fondly, recog-
nizing too late that he had been one of my fathers;
we talked; we posed for pictures. Suddenly, while my
eyes were still dazzled from the glare of the flash
bulbs, I realized that when I had been running down
the lane to pound on Jake's refrigerator door, a be-
havior that always produced a laugh and a bowl of
ice cream, he had been not an old man at all, but
somebody my age!

Some surprise always lurks in the familiar, some
bit of history one can appreciate only with the passing of time and by comparison with the particulars of
a thing intimately known—a person, or community,
or place. The surprise of the familiar is a deeper and
truer discovery than the surprise of the exotic or
strange because it is the kind of surprise that enlarges
our sense of connectedness, rather than that of our
separateness.

This distinction is frequently lost in the endless
preoccupation we now have with matters of self-
esteem. Esteem comes from the knowledge of belonging, not from the fractures of difference. Our deepest

longing is to have a place—in the family, in the community, in the culture, in the world. This is why adolescence is such a torment. It is the time of life when
our need to understand ourselves as individuals necessarily overwhelms our sense of ourselves as ordinary. We are obliged, for that time, to concentrate
on the things that distinguish us from the crowd. We
find ourselves, in consequence, isolated, alienated,
humiliatingly conspicuous. Some cultures, but not
ours, have sympathized with the wretchedness of this
work by offering their youngsters, at the end of this
trial by separation, a ritual way of reestablishing
connections, especially the most fundamental one,
the connection with nature.

This, as I understand it, is what the vision quests
of the Plains Indians were about. A native child was
sent alone to a sacred place for three or four days to
await, in silence and in fasting, a vision from the
spirit world of nature. The vision came not from inside, but from without. It came in the form of a bear,
or a crow, or a snake—in the form of some other *creature*—from whom one took one's name, in whom one
found the spirit of one's life-work, and with whom
one was allied for the rest of one's days. The vision
named you as an individual—it gave you claim of special standing in the community of the tribe—but it
also, and more importantly, affirmed you as a member in good standing of the community at large, the
community of nature. It was a way of marrying into
the world.

When one has a home-place and takes the idea of

it seriously, when one feels bound to it and responsible to it for a lifetime, then one has, in the same way, undertaken the adult work of living both as an individual with unique qualities *and* as a citizen of the commonwealth of a place, with all of the connections that implies: to other individuals, to the whole community of the place, to the work of the place, and to the land itself; and it is this sense of being joined to something good and whole that gives one the confidence, the esteem, necessary to persevere. The conviction is possible then that one does not stand alone. And out of that conviction emerges also the prospect of an endless unfolding of surprises, surprises that reveal the intricacy, and diversity, and invincibility of our ties to all of creation.

Now my tent has become a kind of home-place, an anchor to return to in the evenings wherever I wander, a link with all of the sessions I have held in wild places, and a reminder of my human limits: "Even nomads live within boundaries," Gary Snyder says.

After the tent has been pitched, water must be gathered and filtered or boiled. I filter mine, preferring its taste to that of boiled water, which seems to me to go flat, like old beer, in the purifying heat. It is the one camp duty that seems to me a chore, perhaps because it is necessary at all. Even fifty years ago, I might have dispensed with it, but by now our world is generally contaminated, including all of its waters.

There are signs at the entrances to the canoe country these days warning you against eating too

THE GRACE OF THE WILD · 63

many fish. The fish carry in their flesh concentra-
tions of mercury and other toxic metals that have
drifted in the atmosphere from distant industrial
sites and precipitated in the rainfall. One once went,
like Thoreau, to the wilderness to be freed and puri-
fied. Freedoms and purifications of the soul are still
to be found there, but the body cannot now escape
the transgressions of our industrial labors.

After the water has been rendered drinkable,
there will be, if one's travels have ended at a merciful
hour, time to sit against a boulder or the trunk of a
tree, writing in a journal perhaps, or reading a book
(although I find that I lose my appetite for books in
the wilderness), or surveying the scene, or daydreaming: time to play in the mind, which is frisky after a
day of physical labor. There will be time for a jigger
of brandy, raw in the throat and warm in the belly.

Then a fire must be laid, or the stove (which I
always use) must be lit and a supper prepared.
Canoeing affords mealtime luxuries not possible to
backpackers, but I have become so accustomed to
trail food over the years that I now prefer it: a bowl
of steaming soup; a dish of noodles or rice and a
simple sauce; a salad, when the right materials are
at hand, gathered from near the campsite, cattail
fronds, perhaps, with fiddleheads or mushrooms;
maybe some bannock, studded with berries if they
are ripe; sometimes a package of freeze-dried ice
cream, one of the benefits of technology that I
enthusiastically endorse. Afterwards, something
hot to drink, usually chocolate, but on occasion a

cup of Tang or lemonade. Extravagant meals are unnecessary in the wilderness. The humblest fare, when
you have been active out-of-doors all day, invariably
tastes like a feast. Food never seems closer to sacra-
ment than then.

When I turn off the stove after the water for drinks
has come to a boil, I am freshly reminded of the stark
silence of the wilderness. The tiny flame hissing
beneath the pot makes a noise that would scarcely
be audible in any other setting; here it seems, when
it has been suddenly extinguished, as if it had been
emitting a mighty roar.

The dishes must be washed and packed away with
the foodstuffs in a sack, and the sack must be hung
from a line secured between two trees downwind of
the camp so that the bears can't get at it. This brings
the domestic labors of the day to a close. The per-
formance of these chores lies at the heart of the
wilderness experience: the work gives us common
standing with the rest of life. The squirrel gathering
pine cones for the winter midden, the mother bear
browsing berries with its cub on the ridgetop, the
father osprey flying back to the nest with a bass
skewered in its talons, may be wild, may be in many
particulars incomprehensible to us, but they also,
like us, are bound to their daily chores. It is in our
mutual roles as domestics that our lives most clearly
converge.

By then, whatever wind has been blowing will
have died, and the surface of the lake will have become like glass. This is the time for a last turn in

the canoe, gliding slowly, noiselessly across the
smooth waters, drifting atop the mirror image of forest and sky while the mayflies hatch, and the fish
surface to feed upon them, and the families of ducks
take a social swim, and the sweet coolness of evening
rises in the air.

As you return to camp at the edge of dusk, water
and sky have taken on a pink and mauve glow. You
beach the canoe. You change into a long-sleeved shirt
and long pants: now the mosquitoes, even if they
have been absent all day long, appear suddenly in
energetic masses. They drone an ostinato to bring
down the sun. With the mosquitoes come the dragonflies. They dart up and down the shoreline, their
legs folded into baskets to gather the mosquitoes,
skimming the surface of the water and swooping
skyward again like kites, their wings clacking. Now
and then, if one watches closely, one can also see
the shadowy form of a bat winging at high speed out
toward the lake, intent on sharing in the bounty.
The mosquitoes never stay for long. By the time the
trees on the opposite shore have turned from green
to black, they will have gone again into hiding.
It is as if they are as compelled as we to attend to
the fall of the night.

The blue in the dome of the sky deepens to the
color of cobalt. The line of trees across the water
loses not only its color but also its shape. The distinction between earth and heaven blurs, then disappears. The first star appears, then another, and
another.

I sit on a rock at the edge of the water in the gathering darkness, staring into the depths of the lake and thinking of something Thoreau said, when he was perhaps in a similar mood, about Walden Pond: "A lake," he said, "is the landscape's most beautiful and expressive feature. It is earth's eye; looking into which the beholder measures the depth of his own nature."

Down the lake a solitary loon cries. The sound is low and mournful. It is sometimes mistaken for the howl of a wolf. I think that the cry might have come from my own heart. When it echoes back across the water, it also echoes inside me, and the reverberations do not die away. I shiver, and button my wool shirt, and pull a jacket over it, but I think it is not the sudden coldness alone that stirs within me.

In a few months I will be as old as my father was when he died. I can see him now, looking up at me out of the depths of the lake. He is smiling. He always wanted to be in a place like this, but he never found the time or the means to get here. I see that it did not matter, that he is here now, and always was.

Forty-seven years was the span of his life. Thoreau was forty-five when he died. This rock has been here for two billion years. Somewhere, loons have been crying for a hundred million years. There were already loons when this shore I sit upon was still buried within the heart of a great mountain. Long before the Rocky Mountains, there were loons. Somewhere a wolf is prowling. I can feel it in my bones. I can feel the vibrations in this stone. Thirty million years ago there were wolves. In an hour, I will hear one howling. Before the ice came, it was already howling. Nine thousand years ago, this lake was here. Eight thousand years ago, on a night very like this one, perhaps, an ancestor of mine sat upon this boulder, or on one nearby. A loon was crying, and its cry echoed across these waters, and the echo reverberated in my kin's heart, and it reverberates still.

Tonight, I have a session with myself. I look into the eye of the earth, and I find there myriad things coming forth and expressing themselves: flowers, poets, fathers, lakes, mountains, wolves, loons, boulders of granite, both inside my body and out of it. I have found, after all, the thing I was looking for, the home-place. It is here, I see, everywhere and inside me, where it always was.

I rise, go up the hill, and build a fire against the chill and the darkness. It crackles and spits. Idly I stir a stick in the coals until it glows, and wave it, writing a neon dance in the night. I stare absent-mindedly into the blue and orange flames, hypnotized by them in the ancient way, feeling myself letting go of my body. My eyelids begin to droop, neither with weariness, nor with sleepiness, but with peace.

When the fire has burned itself down, I bank the coals and turn in. At first the sleeping bag feels clammy and chill, but it warms quickly. It is good to be confined within the bag after so much movement, good to be in the embrace again of solid ground after so much water. I turn once or twice or three times, discover the way my body fits best against the contours of the ground, and close my eyes, hoping that I might awaken in the night to hear gentle rain against the fly of the tent or the lapping of water against rock. Then I might fall asleep a second time, a proper lullaby in my ears, bringing gentle dreams.

COMPLINE

The Last Hour of the Day: Loons, Wolves, Night Sounds, Sleep

Sometimes on a cloudy night the canoe country turns as dark as the bottom of the sea. It is impossible then to see your hand in front of your face. You lie in this utter darkness, feeling the hardness of the earth in your hip bones and shoulder blades. You have never been more aware of being entirely alone.

Across the lake, a wolf howls. It is not so much a howl as a wail, a long lament, not languorous but full-toned and intense. The wolf has a tenor voice. It carries operatically across the lake, dies away, echoes back upon itself.

OoooooooooooooooooooooOOOOooo.

You do not stir, but your skin tingles. Some wild part of you desires to rise up and give answer. But from far away comes a better reply, three high trumpet-like notes on an ascending scale.

Ah! Ah! Ah!

On lakes near and far, the loons, hearing the primordial cry, voice their own response, a tumultuous laughter, ecstatic, echoing across all the hard surfaces of this land of rock and water.

A long silence, and then the wail again. And the same answer. And the same ecstatic laughter, deep

throated and joyous. You have never heard music
to equal it. It croons you into a dreamy half-sleep.

Later—you do not know how much later, time
seeming to have vanished in the darkness of the
night—you are abruptly awakened by a loud noise. It
sounds about ten feet from your ear, made by some
living creature, a snort or grunt or perhaps a sneeze.
You bolt upright in your sleeping bag, your heart
pounding, your mouth gone dry, trying not to breathe
audibly, listening through the pores of your skin. You
hear only an eerie silence. You reach for your flashlight, train its beam across the little clearing in the
forest where you are camped. Nothing glitters back at
you; only the dull gray radiance of bark and matted
needles and mosses reflects in the light-thirsty night.

You switch off the flashlight. It seems darker now
than ever. You lie down again, but you do not sleep.
Every particle of you awaits some further sign from
the mysterious companion who has come to share
the night with you. You hear every snapping twig,
every rustling leaf, every lap of water.

You finally drift into the sleep that will hold
you until morning. When you have descended into
dreams, when your body functions according to its
preconscious will, as it has operated through all the
millenia of humankind, when you have abandoned
yourself fearlessly, automatically, to whatever the
night and the forest might bring: then you come
as near to wildness, to a life in nature, as any human can.

"The civil wilderness of sleep," Robert Herrick
called it. You cannot know, when you enter it,

whether you will ever return. It was like that for my father. One evening he slept, and after that the mornings, for him, ceased to rise, although many times since, high in the sky and in watery depths, I am quite sure that I have caught glimpses of him. He seems to be awake still, more awake, perhaps, than ever. "There is more day to dawn," Thoreau said. "The sun is but a morning star."

Somewhere a squirrel flies, and somewhere the moon glows, and you sleep. Somewhere a beaver swims, and somewhere a fisher hunts, and you sleep. Somewhere a night breeze stirs. Somewhere an owl rides upon it, and you sleep. Your face has fallen, and somewhere the stars have risen. Your face has fallen into innocence. For this little while, at least, you can do no harm. You look it; you look young and harmless, as if you might never again be streetwise and carelessly knowing. "Praise ignorance," Wendell Berry's Mad Farmer advises, "for what man has not encountered he has not destroyed."

Somewhere the stars have risen, all hundred million of them in this galaxy, one of a hundred million galaxies. Somewhere there among them you sleep, and dream. You dream of Robert Frost demanding of the fairest star in sight that it speak. And, although loftily reticent, it does say something in the end; it asks of you a certain height.

Somewhere the vegetable mold is becoming humus. Somewhere your own heart is beating. Somewhere the sun is shining. Somewhere your mind is dreaming, and your body is inside your dream, and

you sleep. Somewhere mists are rising and birds are
stirring, and still you sleep.

Everywhere everything is changing. Everything is
in a state of becoming. When the day dawns, it will
be a new day. When the day dawns, there will be a
new you. Your hair is lengthening, your brain is slak-
ing cells, your body is being cleansed and refurbished.
You sleep and you cease to be and you start becoming. You look as innocent as a baby, and you sleep like
one, as well you might. You *are* momentarily innocent, risen in the ethereal air of sleep to a suitable
height. You are only being. You are only becoming.
You *look* becoming.

You waken. It is light. Birds chirp in the forest undergrowth and in its canopy. You crawl from your tent
and stand in the sharp, clean-smelling morning air.
Fog shrouds the lake. The island across the way
seems to be floating in it. You light your stove and
boil a pot of coffee. A chipmunk warily advances to
investigate the intrusion. You find a rock to lean
against, drinking in the stillness with the coffee. You
feel, suddenly, invisible.

You have vanished into the forest, taken a proper
place in it. You stand there belonging, anointed with
the heavenly, the homely, grace of wildness.

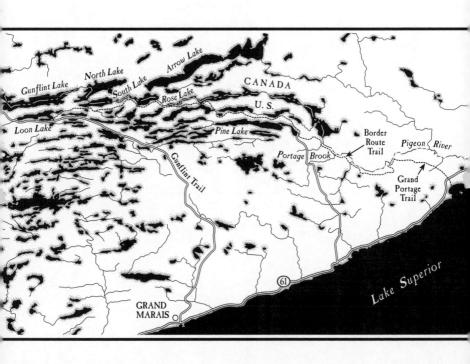

FALL

Walking the Border

Walking
the Border

The sun smiles upon the bay,
upon the tidy village, upon
the great sealake when
we arrive at Grand Portage
in midafternoon, milky
eyed from a long drive.
My friend John Scholl and
I intend to cross the
northeastern corner of the
Boundary Waters Canoe
Area Wilderness, follow the
Minnesota-Ontario border to Fort
Charlotte on the Pigeon River, and take
the Grand Portage Trail from there down
to Lake Superior. This is canoe
country, but, despite my
bum knees, we mean
to walk.

Puddles of water glisten in the streets, and
the path through the last thicket of alders to the
lakeshore is sodden and slick. The country we have
come from was parched all summer, but along Lake
Superior's North Shore the rains have fallen gener-
ously. The wild raspberries are plump, juicy, and
sweet. The leaves have already dropped from the wild
rose bushes, and some of the red-orange hips, sizzling
with color, are almost as big as crab apples. There are
bunchberries and thimbleberries among the brambles,
and pin cherries in the taller thickets. The northern
forest welcomes us with a show of abundance.

Not that John and I think the spectacle is in any
way organized for us. The feast times and famine
times of nature come and go, from the human point
of view, quite capriciously, unintended by any person-
age or force either for our benefit or our harm. Still,
the abundance is there, ours to receive without condition or encumbrance, and this in itself signals our
arrival in a place set apart from the ordinary com-
merce of the world.

We leave the next morning for the trailhead in a fog
so dense that, although it is after nine A.M. when
we start, we need headlights. The fog obscures the
profusion of signs along the way, advertising outfit-
ters, lodges, chapels, bed and breakfasts, eateries,
resorts. The signs remind us that although the
Boundary Waters may be called a wilderness, it is
hardly remote or undiscovered and has not been
so for centuries. The statistic is astounding: one of

every ten wilderness trips in the contiguous forty-
eight United States is into the Boundary Waters.

John has secured the necessary permit for our
entry, and we will conscientiously observe the long
list of rules accompanying it, regulations necessary
to preserve some semblance of wildness in this
much-frequented place.

I think, by contrast, of a canoe excursion my friend
Bill Keitel and I made down the Rock River in southwestern Minnesota one spring day a few months
earlier. Southwestern Minnesota is as little wild as
a place can be. It is sparsely populated, but its lands
are as extensively domesticated—for agricultural
purposes—as those of any big city. The unfarmable
Rock River remains the thinnest possible margin
of wildness in an otherwise industrialized landscape.

The narrow, shallow Rock is, moreover, nobody's
idea of a recreational river. Even on the high-water
day when we negotiated it we frequently had to climb
out of our canoe and pull it across the sandbars from
pool to pool. Brown, lethargic, and rimmed with
low mud banks, the river runs through unscenic
cow pastures and cornfields.

We floated and waded down the Rock that lazy
afternoon, led by a merganser, entertained by flocks
of ruddy turnstones flying in flashing formation,
greeted twice by great horned owls, never once crossing a road or encountering another human being.
When we hauled out of the river above the power
plant at Luverne in the lengthening shadows of early

evening, we could honestly say that we had been somewhere rare and undiscovered.

At the turnoff to Loon Lake, John and I leave the Gunflint Trail, pass the Loon Lake Lodge, and park the car in a grassy lot along a powerline clearing. Halfway up a steep, muddy hill we find a toppled sign marking the Border Route Trail and plunge into the forest. The walk to Topper Lake, just four-and-a-half miles away, is uncomplicated. We reach it by early afternoon. John wants to try his rod at the trout, and we are determined, for once, to have an easy first day. But when we locate the designated campsite—a sheltered ledge a dozen feet above the lake, equipped with such comforts as a pit toilet, log benches, and a metal fire grate—and put down our packs, we discover that the rope we have brought to hang our food sacks out of reach of the bears has vanished. The rope began the hike tied to a strap on my pack. It must have gotten caught on a snag along the trail, and it does not seem wise to try to do without it. We turn back in search of it.

Three young hikers—two men and a woman, one short and stout, one tall and spindly, the third of moderate proportions—hail us as we step back onto the trail.

"A rope?" the tall one says. "Yeah, we saw a rope hanging from a shrub. How far back was it? Two, three miles?"

"No," says the short one. "Can't be that far. We

just saw it fifteen, twenty minutes ago. Isn't that right?" he says to the middle-sized one.

"Don't remember," she says.

Of course, the tall one is right. Our short jaunt turns into a ten-mile march, the last of it taken at temper-tantrum pace.

Still, it is hard to stay out of sorts for long in canoe country. Toward evening, back in camp again, we soak in the cool lake, dry ourselves in the last rays of the sunlight, dine on a stew of chicken or beef—one piece of freeze-dried rubber tastes pretty much like another—and loll in the twilight, watching the trout, too far out to be fished, rising briefly to a small hatch of mayflies. The resident loon patrols the opposite bay like an overlord.

In the middle of the night it rains, but not hard. The patter of raindrops on a tent fly in the depths of the night is as soothing to me as a ride in a car is to a baby. Later the loons begin to laugh, and in the distance a lone wolf howls. Finally the silence of deep night falls, and then, in the hour before dawn, the first songbirds stir, chirping and twittering.

Although the morning dawns gray and ominous, John correctly predicts that the clouds will dissipate in the heat of the day. The whine of truck tires on the pavement of the Gunflint Trail wafts like smoke over the forest. We are eager to put this intrusion behind us.

Not far from Topper Lake we come to an intersection in the trail. There is a signpost; we have merely to follow the proper arrow. We will wonder later whether the signpost was out of alignment or whether we had simply misread it, but we will not wonder enough to go back and look at it again.

We walk for an hour, come to another intersection, one we haven't expected but which, when we consult the map, seems plausible. We take the fork headed east, the direction we want to travel. Thirty minutes later we encounter still another intersection. We veer eastward again on an old logging road. Much of this country was logged at the turn of the century, and it is still laced with leftover roads. By and by, the road skirts the shore of a marshy lake. We expect just such a lake, but on our right, not our left. In another hour it has become unavoidably obvious that the route we are following is not the Border Route Trail.

We retrace our steps, annoyed for the lost time, for the extra miles, and for what we are missing: you see and hear almost nothing in the distraction of being off course, which is one reason why a person who is a little lost often becomes hopelessly so.

We stop for lunch at the intersection just after the one, we later deduce, where we made our wrong turn. A tentative exploration of the trail in the direction we did not take rules it out: it leads to a clear-cut and then turns south toward the Gunflint.

Just when we resolve to retrace our steps even farther, the three students we met the day before— they are on a last fling before the start of classes at the University of Minnesota-Duluth—step into view.

"Fancy meeting you again!" the tall one says.

"Where are you headed?" the short one asks.

"We wish we knew," John says.

"We took a wrong turn somewhere," I explain, "and we've spent all morning trying to find our way back to the main trail."

"No problem," the middle-sized one says. "We're camped at Sock Lake, which is just down the ridge from the main trail. Want us to show you how to get there?"

"Maybe you could just point the way."

"Don't know that we could," the tall one says, laughing. "Better let us come with you. We've got nothing better to do anyway."

We trudge off sheepishly after them, and, by and by, come upon a marshy little lake. But the trail around the end of it has been flooded by a beaver dam, which looks too narrow to cross.

"Well, I'll be damned," the short one says. "Never seen this place before."

We circle back once more, make a new start, arriving eventually at Sock Lake, where our guides are camped. They have been enjoying the comings and goings of a family of otters, they say. The tall one produces a book and curls up with it against a tree. The short one stretches out in the sun. The middle-sized one swirls fruit drink mix in a jug of water. They look as contented as otters.

A sweaty hike carries us through thickets of fallen timber from the south shore of the lake to the point on its northern shore where a spur trail leads up to the main one. We pause to catch our breath, bid the student who has accompanied us a grateful farewell, climb a steep ridge, and finally achieve the spot we have been trying to reach for the last six hours. We are now half a mile from the camp at which we began the morning.

The joy has gone out of the day. We walk gloomily for fifteen or twenty minutes and come to the shores of a marshy little lake. This time we recognize it as Mucker Lake, the same one we have already passed three times from two other directions. Its familiarity does not gladden our hearts.

Early in the evening, bushed, we make camp in a grove of tall cedars along Partridge Lake. The place nestles in a bowl, surrounded on all sides by dense thickets of forest undergrowth, sheltered from above by the canopy of the cedars, carpeted in a thick, dark mat of needles. Such a place would strike some as like a cathedral, but it seems to me more like a Victorian parlor, too dark, too heavily furnished, too constricted, too gloomy. I feel claustrophobic.

The lake is shallow, mud bottomed, and comparatively warm, not an inviting place to swim, and even from the narrow opening along the lakeshore there is scarcely a view. In the premature twilight of the forest we cook another pot of something rubbery and anonymous. John disappears with his fly rod. I poke absentmindedly at a Sierra cup full of stew and in my lethargy drop my spoon. It falls under a log behind the stump on which the gas stove sits. A pan of water boils on the stove.

Too weary to think of walking around the stump,
I try to move it without first setting aside the pan of
boiling water that is balanced precariously atop it. The
stump balks and then budges abruptly. The pan tips.

Scalding water pours over my bare left forearm,
searing it. The sudden surge of pain is excruciating.
I drag myself down to the lake and thrust my scalded
limb into the water. The coolness quenches the pain.
The burn is bearable, I find, if I soak it for half a
minute out of every three or four. But half an hour
into this therapy, when I pull my arm from the water,
a fat leech dangles from the tenderest part of the
burn. I can tolerate leeches, but the impertinence
of this particular leech enrages me. I slap at it hard,
doubling my pain. After that I apply a medicated
salve to the wound and bite my lip and smoke two
cigars to distract myself from the fire in my arm
and from the tears involuntarily welling in my eyes.

John returns. "The sunset is spectacular tonight,"
he says. "You ought to come and look it."

"I've seen sunsets," I snap.

Heavy clouds roll in, and when the darkness falls,
it is total, darker than blindness. I raise my good arm
until my hand touches my nose, but I am lost to myself. Under cover of this blackness, I fall mercifully
into quick, deep sleep.

The next morning begins in sunshine. Our enclave
among the cedars, three hundred feet below the
high ridge on which we intend to walk for the day,
seems almost cheerful in the dappled light. My arm,

although tender to the touch, looks only as if it has
been severely sunburned. The pain has vanished. It
is going to be a splendid day for hiking.

We climb the ridge and head east, walking where,
ages ago, mountains stood. The sensation is, in fact,
like traversing the rugged foothills of a great mountain range. The ridge lays at an elevation of about two
thousand feet. The lakes to the north of us run in a
chain in a narrow valley five hundred feet deep, and
beyond them rise the forested peaks of the Canadian
wilds, stretching all the way to the Arctic.

Much of the way, we walk in the understory of
spruces and white pines. My eyes are drawn to the
forest floor. Funguses sprout everywhere in every
shape and size and color: pink, orange, red, yellow,
ivory, brown, even pale green. I recognize puffballs,
club mushrooms, amanitas, oyster mushrooms,
members of the *Hypomyces* and *Lentinus* genuses.
There are many others whose names I don't know.

Where the sunlight regularly reaches the forest
floor the trail is bordered by thickets of waist-high
thimbleberries, a bramble with handsome palmate
leaves like those of the maple, deeply green, and as
much as eight inches across. The plant, a member
of the rose family, is also known as the flowering
raspberry. Its fruits, mounted on a stalk at the top
of the plant, are orange-red (the same color as rose
hips but less intense) and have a bland, sweet flavor
that is cloying at first, and vaguely off in its taste,
as if it were just beginning to rot, and then addicting.

In shadier places bunchberries grow just as

thickly, although they stand only a few inches high, their prominently veined, egg-shaped leaves marking them as relatives of the dogwoods. They are elegant plants in every season, formal and tidy. In spring and early summer they bear spotlessly white flowers. In early fall they produce clusters of scarlet berries on stalks above their vibrantly green leaves, ornamenting the forest floor as if for Christmas. Later, the leaves themselves will turn scarlet, making a splash of color brighter than any in the forest canopy.

In the understory of these tall northern forests I see large-leaved asters with their ghostly pale flowers, the heart-shaped leaves of the Canada mayflowers, false Solomon's seals, wood anemones, strawberries, red raspberries, currants.

And there are many nonflowering plants, which filigree the boreal forest floor: ferns, club mosses, horsetails, feather mosses, and reindeer moss, a pale gray-green lichen, actually.

Occasionally, on some high, rocky knoll along the ridge, the forest opens, making a courtyard, never much bigger than a basketball floor. There flourish raspberries and strawberries, tall grasses, and great masses of purple and white flowers. The purple ones are red-stalked asters and Lindley's asters, the white ones pearly everlastings. The pearly everlasting is one of the many plants that high mountains and the north woods share. It gets its euphonious name from its integrity as a dried specimen; it looks much the same dead or alive, owing in part to the hairy foliage that protects it from the cold and gives it, even when it is alive, a gray, almost silvery cast, a pallid greenness.

We have come too early for the brilliant autumnal yellowing of the aspens and birches. Those golden yellows occur when the trees stop the production of chlorophyll in preparation for winter and the supplies that remain in the outer layers of the leaves are consumed, revealing the fundamental pigments underneath (they have been present all along)—carotene, the same pigment that in larger doses makes carrots orange; and xanthophyll, which also colors egg yolks and canary feathers.

But we have arrived in time to see the first fiery reds of fall in the leaves of two small, almost shrubby, hardwoods characteristic of the north woods forest, the mountain ashes and the mountain, or moose, maples. The reds are produced by anthocyanins, coloring agents in the sap—the same ones that tint apples and red cabbages. They are activated by the exposure to sunlight after the chlorophyll in the leaves has been used up. Not many of the trees have yet turned, but it takes only a specimen or two to light up a forest vista. At every bend of the trail we are freshly assaulted with the brilliant news of fall.

We walk for hours absorbed in this richly appointed miniature world—the forest that is four feet high hiding in the shadow of the one a hundred feet high. Then we round a curve in the trail and suddenly find ourselves on the pinnacle of a towering red-brown palisade, the jagged cliff plunging straight down fifty stories into blue lakes: South Lake, Rat

Lake, Rose Lake, snaking away west and east beyond
sight.

The lakes are part of what was once a great highway. They rang with the songs of the voyageurs, those
Frenchmen—small as jockeys so that they could fit
into the crowded canoes—who rented themselves out
as beasts of burden to the fur trade in the last century
and the one before it, provisioned only with lard and
corn and tobacco and sustained by what? Sustained
perhaps by what Edward Hoagland calls "the jubila-
tion of discovery," the thrill forever lost even in our
wildernesses of going where others have never been
before, of seeing and hearing and smelling things
previously known only to God.

The highway that ran this way was three thousand miles long. It penetrated the heart of a continent, laying open some of the wildest and most
beautiful places on earth. To have been at home in
all of it, as the voyageurs, and the Native Americans
before them, were! Standing at the head of the
palisade looking out over the vast green and blue
remains of that old kingdom, I can conjure its linger-
ing allure. I can almost imagine why you would vol-
unteer to break your back to be part of it.

Laurens Van Der Post, an explorer of Africa, once
observed that we have become adept in our century at
knowing things. But the secret to fulfillment, he re-
marked, lies not in knowing but in being known. He
had in mind not fame but the sense of well-being that
comes from having presented yourself to the world,
to the whole world, to the wild parts of it as much as

the settled. He meant the security that comes from not being a stranger, as we are to so much of life. "Mr. Griswold owns all the property in America," the poet Corita Kent scoffed, "but the trees never heard of him." We know a lot of things, I think, standing in the suddenly chill wind of the high north woods, but most of us—even the best of us—are unknown here. Is it any wonder that we feel a nagging loneliness in the face of nature?

A stream cuts between Duncan and Rose Lakes in the northeastern corner of the Boundary Waters Canoe Area. At the intersection of the trail and the stream a waterfall, perhaps thirty feet high, hides in a granite cove overshadowed by tall pines. The sound of falling water resonates against the rocks so soothingly that the impulse to throw off your boots, curl up nearby in a bed of pine needles, and doze away the day is almost overwhelming. The place has the same cozy feeling as the odd corner of a rambling house on a stay-at-home Sunday afternoon. The water sprays out of the basin that receives the falls, nourishing a little rain forest community on the rock ledges rising above it. Ferns and emerald green mosses and rose-colored mushrooms flourish there, miniatures all, each hung with a necklace of pearl-shaped water drops.

To the north, beyond the waterfall, the land plunges steeply into Rose Lake. Here lurks the real surprise of this place. There is a portage trail between the two lakes, the steepest part of it eased by, of all things, a sturdy cedar-log staircase miles from any road, broad and deep, handsomely made. There are 119 steps. They were built by the Civilian Conservation Corps in the 1930s.

We climb the stairs, still sturdy after half a century of abuse from the weather and the tramplings of tens of thousands of pairs of boots. Halfway up we pause to catch our breath.

"You know, there's hardly a place in Minnesota that doesn't still benefit from some Depression-era public works project," I say. "Dams, roads, sidewalks, picnic shelters, swimming beaches, buildings, rip-rapped lakeshores and river banks—it's really an incredible legacy."

"It's amazing what we could afford when we didn't have any money," John said. "This staircase in the middle of a wilderness, for one thing."

"We're having the longest economic expansion in our history, and volunteers have to keep this trail open because there's no public money to do it."

"And back home we're laying off teachers and complaining about welfare moms and reducing hours at the public library. It's hard to be rich, I guess."

I think about John's shrewd comment. If you've got wealth, you've got to protect it, worry about it, fret about taxes, keep track of it. Rich people spend a lot of psychic energy that poor folks don't have to pay. Maybe that's why poor people are more generous than rich people.

I ask John, "Did you see that Gallup poll the other day that found that half of all the charitable giving in this country is by people making less than $30,000 a year?"

"It didn't surprise me," he says. "You and I both know where the money comes from to support our church, and it's not, by and large, from the people who have the most to give."

"Well, there are some big donors. I guess you just have to be rich enough."

"Be honest, Paul. Do you know anybody who feels rich enough?"

We climb the last seventy-five stairs, reach the top of the ridge, and walk until we come to a rocky opening with a fine ledge for a bench, a breeze, and a view across Rose Lake into Canada. There we take off our packs and pause for lunch—cheese and crackers, beef jerky, dried apples, candy bars.

"While we were walking," I tell John, "I was thinking about something that happened when Nancy and I were still newlyweds, both in college and living on practically nothing. One evening we got into Clyde, our ancient Plymouth, the car Nancy's aunt gave us, and went to the grocery store to buy milk for the cat. We wanted to buy something for ourselves too, but we only had enough money for milk, and we couldn't let the cat starve. On the way, a drunk roared through a red light and smashed into Clyde. We got out to inspect the damage. The right rear fender of the car was battered but the wheel still turned. The drunk, who wanted nothing to do with the cops, offered us twenty-five dollars in cash to forget the whole thing.

We took the money, sped off to the grocery store, giddy with our good fortune, and bought not only milk but the fixings for a great party, and a great party it was.

"I figure our income last year was about forty-seven times that of the first year of our marriage, so an equivalent windfall for us now would be $1,175, if I've done the math in my head right. And you know what? If we got such a windfall now, I don't think our first instinct would be to throw a party or make a donation to charity. We'd call Tom, our stock broker, and ask him to find us a good investment."

We put away our lunch things, take up our packs, and head down the trail again. It is midafternoon, and the rays of the sun have begun to lengthen. They pierce the canopy of the forest, making it seem haloed. Sweat trickles down the small of my back, a feeling I've always liked.

As we walk on, I make, as I do more often than I would like to admit when I am walking, a little speech to myself. Charity, I tell myself, is a private pleasure, but justice requires the hard labor of a community. Talk all you like about how the maid's pennies are the moral equivalent of Donald Trump's millions; the practical fact is that the difference between them is a very large sum of money and everything that that difference can buy, including, not incidentally, status, influence, and fame. And what of those who stand in need of justice, who are to be the recipients and not the dispensers of charity? To make the work of justice the business of the community, rather than of private largesse, is to spread the responsibility in ways that ennoble both those who give and those who receive. This dichotomy can be reduced to its essential pronouns. Charity is for them. Justice is for us.

Left to our individual whims, I think, my internal voice rising, we will never do the work of justice because we are too rich to see how we can afford it. Either we practice justice out of the discipline of the collective will, or we don't practice it at all. For the moment, we choose private over public ambition. Richer than ever by our own accounting, we can no longer afford houses for the homeless, or books for our libraries, or decent schools for our children.

There was a time only half a century ago when, in our destitution, we could afford not only these things but also things so out of the way as staircases between wilderness lakes. I do not, I remind myself, despair for the future; we will be able to afford them again, I am certain, just as soon as we are poor enough to be unable to do without them.

And then I stumble over a big boulder in the trail, teeter, and fall against a tree, which is what happens to hikers who are making speeches rather than watching their feet.

"Are you okay?" John asks.

"I think I'm over it now."

We climb to a crest on the ridge just south of the border between Ontario and Minnesota, round a bend in the trail, and emerge upon an opening in the forest.

An enormous man kneeling before a semicircular
cache of stones rises and turns to greet us. He is cos-
tumed from head to toe in camouflage that makes
him conspicuous. He seems as surprised to see us as
we are him.

"Hunting bear," he says.

We nod.

"This is my bait here," he says, pointing to a coffee can at the center of the cache of stones, which
looks like a crude altar. It reminds me of the trap sets
for cougars that I have seen in the Montana mountains. I doubt the wisdom of luring bears to a blind
curve on a public trail, but I say nothing.

"We tested the site a couple of weeks ago and
brought two of 'em in," the man says. He seems eager
to make conversation. He must think us an odd pair
when we merely nod again, bid him good day, cross
the knoll, and reenter the forest.

Once I would have been enchanted by the prospect
of a bear hunt. I was a boy then. I dreamed that one
day I would construct a wilderness hermitage and
pass my days in splendid solitude, living off the land
by my wits, trapping and hunting to earn the little
money I would need. Two or three times, in fact, I
left the family house and set up camp along the big
slough at the north end of our farm, announcing that
the time had come for me to make my way as a wild
man. I had not yet reached puberty. Once I stuck it
out for three days and three nights, but I had been reduced by then to a diet of green field corn and boiled
leopard frogs, and the ground had grown hard and the

nights lonely and frightening. I trudged home dispirited. That day the dream of a life of glorious isolation began to fade, although I suppose it didn't entirely die until the day I fell in love.

The truth is, I was never much of a hunter. I was a lousy shot. But long after I had ceased to plan for my reversion to wildness, I was a determined and ultimately successful trapper. There seems to be a widespread instinct in boys at the age of pubescence— in rural boys at any rate—to undertake shooting or trapping as a rite of passage. And it does seem an uncanny act of cultural recapitulation. The age at which boys become trappers, I notice, is precisely the age at which, in preagricultural societies, they would have left behind childish pursuits to take up the adult labor of hunting.

If you would be a successful hunter or trapper— this is especially true of trapping—you must learn something significant about your prey: about its habits, its diet, its sensory acuities, about the patterns and methods of its life. You will need to learn how to read a landscape, deciphering the clues it offers to the mostly covert lives of its wild inhabitants: how to distinguish a track and to reconstruct the story it tells, to identify a tuft of hair, to decode the information in a pile of scat. In learning these things you will find yourself drawn, bit by bit, into the interior lives of your prey.

You learn in trying to think like a fox or a mink, even if it is ultimately for the purpose of entrapment, that the task is tougher than you have imagined. You

match wits against a dumb animal—some would say
a creature with a hard-wired brain, incapable of anything like a thought—and you find that the advantage
is not necessarily yours. Any boy who has tried to trap
a fox and who is at all thoughtful about the experience
will be forever rid of the notion of insensible nature.

When I had outgrown the need to hunt but was
still intimately familiar with the countryside around
our farm, I hid away on the opening day of deer-
hunting season and followed the hunt as a partisan
of the deer. It was amusing to me, and tremendously
cheering, to see how cleverly the deer eluded the men
in orange. Very few deer were harvested in our valley
despite their bountiful numbers and the tremen-
dous investment in pursuing them. I cheered for the
pheasants, too, which I saw on every walk across my
domain until the opening day of the hunting season.
Then, as if they could read the calendar, they hun-
kered down. You nearly had to step on one before
it moved, and even when flushed it would often run
through the grass rather than burst into the air, as
at other times of the year, with that great booming
of wings that always makes my heart race.

When the process works in the usual way, a boy
passes through his trapper stage, suddenly grows several inches in one year, and discovers girls. The traps
rust in a dark corner of the garage, the play-soldier
outfits go into the rag bin with the Superman underwear, and a young man dons his first pair of denims
that are not destined to wear out at the knees in three
months. He stands up and gets on with life.

What lingers afterwards is an affectionate, nostalgic memory of long fall afternoons in the out-of-doors, hot on some trail, absorbed in what is essentially—now that we don't hunt for our livelihoods—a difficult game. That, and a certain amount of hard information about natural history not easily acquired in any other way. The good field biologists, the great naturalists, the ardent conservationists, have almost all gotten their start as boys at the butt ends of guns, or carrying wicker packs full of blued traps and bottles of musk oil and the essences of urines.

The other route to a constructive affection for natural life—more common among women than men—is through the sketching pencil. Many of our best female naturalists—Ann Zwinger and Annie Dillard are notable examples—found their way from their drawing boards into nature.

From infancy, a disproportionate amount of what we remember comes to us through our nerve ends. This is why, at one stage of your life, you may not be able to remember your telephone number, but you can recall vividly the Armistice Day storm, and how to milk a cow, which you haven't done for thirty years. You cannot see in your mind's eye even one of the forty-eight scenic overlooks you visited on your last vacation trip, but you can remember in exquisite detail a walk you took one afternoon months, or years, ago.

This is the difference between scenery and place: scenery is something you have merely looked at; place is something you have experienced. A boy in

pursuit of an animal or an artist translating the lip
of a jewelweed flower from eye to paper through the
tips of her fingers is embarked upon a journey out of
a scene and into a place. This voyage into place ultimately leads toward memory, the great leavening
agent of our lives. A memory reverberates and echoes;
it gives height and texture to every new experience.

There came a time in my own trapping life when
I knew my prey well enough that I would rather see
them alive than outsmarted. Affection and respect
overtook the joy of the hunt, and when it did, I, like
most boys, put away my traps, stood up and got on
with life. But I had been permanently changed in the
process. I started as an invincible boy and emerged
as a vulnerable lover.

We pass through the forest and down a portage trail,
leaving behind the bear hunter, and set up camp
along Pine Lake. Sleep is twice delayed. First, just
after we have retired, we are stirred by a peculiar bird
or animal noise that we have been hearing frequently
but have been unable to identify. It is a short, squeak-
ing sound, almost like a scratch, but regular and
rhythmic, percussive. Although a small noise, it carries acutely. This time it comes from just beyond our
tent door. We peer into the twilight and laugh. Neither
of us has come close to guessing the source: a squirrel
extracting nuts from a pine cone.

An hour or two later we are aroused from our
slumber by heavy footsteps and the sound of sticks
cracking sharply. A moose? A bear? I fumble for my

glasses, look out into the night. It is our bear hunter and a companion, brandishing big metal flashlights with powerful beams, chattering drunkenly, bulling their way through the underbrush to the campsite we know to be just up the shore.

In the morning we see that the hunters have eschewed the well-beaten trail ten yards to the south and pioneered their own instead. Every twenty feet all the way to their campsite they have hacked huge scars in the tall pines that grace the lakeshore. It is a gratuitous desecration, but I am not surprised by it. Boys will be boys.

In the morning a fierce wind sweeps out of the north, and the air is damp and penetratingly cold. John and I bundle up in our warmest clothes and set out along the trail, bound for the eastern-most edge of the Boundary Waters Canoe Area. The exertion almost keeps us warm. When we come to the last of the palisades, we are not tempted to linger. Stopping for more than a minute or two brings a chill as suddenly shocking as the afternoon plunges we have been taking into the frigid lakes, lakes surprisingly barren for all the lushness of the forests that embrace them.

Not only the cold invigorates us. Overnight, the cutting edge of winter has arrived. The drama of the turn in the seasons lends urgency to our progress. The simple fact of change, slapping icily at bare skin, prods us to a new degree of wakefulness. Blood rushes to the veins in our wind-blushed cheeks through some process of massive internal roiling, communicating to every deep cell a fresh challenge from the far-flung world. How blessed we are, I think, to have settled into a place so continuously and radically reborn.

By midmorning the wind has switched to the east and the sun has burned away the early haze. We have, in any case, descended by then into the cozy half-light of deep forest, beyond reach of the tempestuous skies. Becalmed, shrouded in quiet, we dreamily walk the sun-dappled forest, lost in that strange and pacific state of being which, although wakeful, is beyond the outer edge of thought. This feeling is as close to pure experience as you ever get, a passage of time unadulterated by judgment or rationale, utterly unselfconscious, wholly physical. The experience is, I suppose, innocent in the way that we think of very young children as innocent. We lack the motive to do any consequential evil. By its timelessness the hour seems to bestow the gift of time. I imagine whimsically that if life could always be like this, it would go on forever.

John is the first to spot the creature that hauls us out of reverie and back into the present. Sleek and fleet, the animal races along the forest floor, hesitates for a fatal moment, and then scurries up a slender spruce tree no more than twenty feet high, too far from the adjacent larger trees, the creature quickly discovers, to afford a leaping escape. When all of us have come to a halt, John and I stand a few yards in front of the spruce, and the pine marten perches in the crotch of a limb near its peak, furtively eyeing the nearest tall tree, flexing its muscles for a jump, deciding against it. The marten flexes twice more, looks desperately about for an alternative. Seeing none, it settles back against the tree and turns its eyes on us.

It is lavishly beautiful, and we are thrilled at making its acquaintance. Once there were tens of thousands of pine martens in these northern forests, and then, like so many creatures, they were reduced to nearly local extinction. Only recently have they begun to flourish again. Three factors conspired against them: their inability to adapt to the second-growth forests that the loggers left behind; their luxurious chocolate brown coats, lucrative to the fur trade; and their inquisitiveness, which made them easy prey for trappers.

The pine marten's gaze is frank and deep. Its eyes are large and dark, as wide-eyed as a baby's. It has a broadly triangular head, disproportionately allocated to eyes, and squat, sharply pointed ears—ears a caricaturist would give to a devil—and it has about it the alertness—the impression of intense energy—that we would call stage presence in an actor. After its initial furtive search for an escape, it seems to have lost its nervousness, but not its concentration.

I was mugged once on a dark street. "Got a match?" a voice behind me asked. I knew instinctively what was meant, although I had never before been mugged, but I hesitated and turned toward my fate anyway. For a

transitory moment I was terrified and in the next instant my brain had calculated the confrontation as
unavoidable. In that instant the sensation of fear vanished, and I could only concentrate on the experience
at hand as if it were the most interesting episode of
my life, as, indeed, in some ways it was.

The mugging could not have lasted more than a
minute or two. I was, fortunately, carrying quite a lot
of money—all the money I had in the world, as a
matter of fact—and the size of the take gratified my
assailants. Did I have anything else? Jewelry? A
watch? I did not, although if I had had a blank check
I would have volunteered to fill it out for any amount.
Nothing else? Nothing. The snub-nosed pistol was
withdrawn from my belly. I was pointed in a direction
I had not intended to go and ordered to retreat slowly,
not looking back or making a sound. I did exactly as
I was told. I walked at least a mile, taking exaggerated
interest in everything I passed but seeing nothing.
I had lost track of time. I might have walked for ten
minutes or half an hour or half a day.

Thinking about it later, I was astonished to realize
how calm I had been. Eventually it dawned on me
that I must be beyond danger. I stopped and turned
very slowly to look back. I saw no one. I ran, then, to
a friend's house nearby and rang the doorbell. He let
me in. I told him too rapidly what had happened. He
went into the kitchen to mix me a drink. I sat on the
couch in the living room. And then I began to tremble
all over violently. I have seldom been so frightened as
I was for the next few minutes in that safe haven.

I wonder if it will be like that for the pine marten. I wonder if the collected stare with which he regards us will give way after we have departed to a paroxysm of fear and trembling, or if he regards us merely as curiosities. Perhaps he makes nothing of us at all, either because he does not have the capacity for analysis or because, like me, he notices only the peripheral details of such an incident. I remember much about my mugging, but the most I can say about my assailants is that they were male, that there were three of them, and that at least one of them had a gun.

Perhaps the pine marten does not really see me, but I see it down to its silken hairs. It is beautiful because it seems so perfectly attuned to its place—in its coloration, its small size, its swiftness and alertness, its thick coat against the wind that has already turned wintry, in its skills as a climber and hunter, and in its large, dark eyes—the creature seems completely at home. It has the grace of living in harmony with its surroundings.

We humans have our own considerable graces, but this harmony is not one of them. Ours is the history of a widening disengagement from the world of nature. We seem not to be able to avoid destructive relationships with the rest of the living world. We stumble awkwardly about, breaking living things, crushing them, unwittingly smothering them, inadvertently scaring them away—often against our best intentions. We are, afoot in the natural world, as gangling and gawky as adolescents.

For this reason the Spanish philosopher José Ortega y Gasset calls hunting a "vacation from the human condition." It is only when animal and human are engaged as hunter and hunted, he argues, that we cease to be fugitive from nature and confront it on its own terms. "The only adequate response to a being that lives obsessed with avoiding capture is to try to catch it," he writes in *Meditations on Hunting.*

So he condemns people like me who have substituted looking for hunting. We are, he says, voyeurs—still hunters, but only idealistically, platonically; we are guilty—the ultimate sin in his view—of affected piety. He does not say it, but his meaning is clear: Hunters with binoculars and cameras are to real hunting as consumers of pornography are to people enagaged in healthy sexual relationships. I have thought about that argument a lot. I want to refute it, but I confess that I am unable to say where the error lies.

And there is the intense discomfort that comes over me as I watch the treed pine marten, the regret at having violated its territory, the overwhelming desire I feel to release it from the bondage in which I hold it by fear.

I look to John and see that he feels the same remorse. We shift our packs and move on down the trail toward the edge of the Boundary Waters, neither looking back nor saying anything for a long time.

We depart the Boundary Waters on the bridge over the outlet between Little John and McFarland Lakes, arriving at a Forest Service campground. We have planned to spend the night there, but it is only mid-day, the campground is unappealingly crowded, it looks dowdy by comparison with our wilderness way stations, and the sun shines brilliantly, enticing us onward. John and I look at each other and shrug. We are agreed: let's press ahead. The map indicates a number of possible campsites along the way; we can stop whenever we like.

In a mile or so the trail disappears into a shambles of downed timber, the legacy of a fierce storm. We are hemmed in on one side by a river that does not look fordable and on the other by swamps. There seems no choice but to lug, as best we can, along the ridge through the deadfalls. We can't take more than a few steps without climbing over or under yet another tree, fiendishly difficult work. We console ourselves with the thought that if the going gets too tough, we can rest at the campsite ahead another mile or two and tackle the route again in the morning, when we are fresh. More than an hour later, soaked in sweat, smothered in grime, snagged and scratched into sullen silence, we conclude to do just that. But either we have missed the campsite, or it is buried in rub-bish, and we have come too far to turn back. The map shows another possibility not far ahead, down the ridge at the edge of a swamp.

We set out again. When we pause to take our bearings, I lean my walking stick against a tree, leave it absentmindedly behind, circle back angrily for it, have trouble locating it, trip, and fall on my

face. I throw a little fit, feel foolish, then better. Soon
after that, John, out of sight, who is as patient as the
day is long, begins to curse loudly. I find him dan-
gling by his pack from the limb of a tree he has tried
to crawl under, impaled like an insect upon a pin.
Smirking, I set him free.

"I'm glad *you're* amused," he says.

In late afternoon, weary to the marrow, we finally
reach the edge of the forest. Ahead of us, across a
little stream, stretches a swamp, overgrown with
shrubs and grasses taller than our heads, through
which a watery trail faintly winds. The campsite,
if there ever was one, is underwater. We look at each
other despairingly, and consult the map again. On
the far edge of the swamp, there is another possibility. "The picnic table at the campsite near Portage
Brook makes a nice resting spot," the trail guide says,
"especially to view the rising mist from the hills
across the river. . . . The cement circle is not for any
strange ritual but for a fire." A picnic table! Rising
mists across the river! A fire ring! Heartened, we
press on. If we hurry, we should be settled before
dark.

The way through the swamp is nearly as miser-
able as the tree-strewn terrain we have just left. We
see nothing except the abundant evidence of bears.
With almost every step, we sink three or four inches
into the muck, at times to our boot tops; we make
progress by doing a few thousand leg lifts. But we
have gotten our second wind; if we have to, we can

slog on until we drop, which might be soon. But not far ahead, we remind ourselves, there is a picnic table from which to watch the night fall. In the west, the sky is beginning to color.

When we reach Portage Brook, we find the picnic table and the fire ring, as advertised. The table is sitting at a cockamamie angle, the fire ring shattered and overgrown with raspberries and young alders. The site has been logged and bulldozed since the guidebook was written. There are not two square feet of level ground anywhere, and even had there been, everything is thickly covered with the shrubby vegetation that volunteers in the first generation after a forest has been cleared. It is obvious long before we quit our aimless search for a place to pitch a tent or spread out a sleeping bag that we will not spend the night there. A narrow, rickety footbridge with a rakish tilt to the east leads across the brook. I suggest that we sleep on it. John is tired enough to entertain the idea for several seconds.

The sun is about to set. There is nothing we can do about it. The sun will have to set if it wants to. We perch on the high end of the picnic table, our packs off, trying not to say anything we will regret later. It occurs to me that it was my idea to go on this hike. I hope that John has forgotten that. Probably he hasn't.

A drink of water will perk us up. But we have exhausted the last of our supply a mile back. I rummage out my filter, which has wormed its way to the very bottom of the pack, as any item you want always will. When I finally reach it, the pump seems to be broken.

Fine, we say through lips bent into imitations of
pleasant grins, since we have to boil water anyway,
we'll have a cup of tea. The water in the brook is already a kind of tea, a deep, reddish brown in color,
steeped in the rotting vegetation of the swamp.
I gather a pot of it while John fires up the stove. As
we are sipping the last of the acidic brew, twilight
descends.

Wordlessly, we help each other into our packs,
cross the brook, from which no enchanting mists are
rising, and climb into the forest again. A mile and a
half ahead, there is supposed to be a road, and near it
there are said to be some campsites. We'll see. The
sky darkens quickly, and the moon has not yet risen.
We trudge by flashlight through the inky forest along
a narrow, slippery trail. We seem to have been hiking
since birth.

We reach the road at 10 P.M. We have been hiking
for almost fourteen hours: seventeen miles up rocky
ridges and down them, over and under a million
deadfalls, through miles of mud. We might as well
have walked seventeen thousand miles. Perhaps we
have. My brain is no longer capable of calculations.

There is a place to camp. It is occupied by a
pickup camper. What the hell. I pitch our tent in a
patch of grass on the shoulder of the road. Perhaps
we'll get lucky and somebody will drive by in the
night and strike us dead. John goes in search of water.
We boil dinner. We are long past hunger, we realize,
but what are we going to do with the food now that it
is cooked? We cram it down, gagging on every bite.

We wash the dishes. We hang our packs. It is eleven. We prepare to go to bed.

But wait. John has forgotten to brush his teeth. I stare at him. He is serious. He wants to brush his teeth. I would kill him if I had the energy. We retrieve the packs. He brushes his teeth. I don't brush mine out of principle. We hang the packs again. We get into our sleeping bags. I am not speaking. We are camped on a big rock which slants toward the bottom of the tent. What the hell. We'll sleep on the damned rock. We'll slide down it into the bottom of the tent all night long. Who gives a shit?

Three years later, in Isle Royale National Park, we slog through another interminable day, wash dishes in the dark, prepare to retire. "I think I'll brush my teeth," John says. He pauses. "Is it all right if I brush my teeth?" A sly little grin crosses his face, just for an instant. I seem not to have heard him.

This is also friendship: We get up the next morning from the bottom of the tent, where we are curled like cutworms, have a (barely) civil breakfast, break camp, and set out for the Pigeon River as if nothing has happened. Not a word about any of it. What would there be to say?

The day is sparkling and pleasantly cool. The first part of the hike is along the road where we have spent the night. Road hiking is murder on knees, and I have a temperamental one. After I climbed Longs Peak in Rocky Mountain National Park, I hobbled for a month. My right knee has begun to throb by the time we cut cross-country again, but I am not complaining. Our destiny has been affirmed: we cannot be defeated.

We strike out across the Superior National Forest toward the Pigeon River. There is more mud, more cross-country hiking through fallen timber. The place where we have planned to camp for the night proves dismal: a patch of scraggy grass and gravel next to a collection of garbage cans that have been tipped by bears and gleaned, but not for much. The scattered debris consists mainly of diapers and beer cans. The diapers and the beer cans both are well chewed. We pass up the place, and soon reach a well-made, meticulously maintained trail through a pleasant forest.

By midafternoon we arrive at Fort Charlotte, now only a name, the physical vestiges of the fort having long since disappeared. It is the place where the voyageurs loaded their canoes after the nearly nine-mile climb, a thousand feet up from Lake Superior, carrying their supplies in 180-pound loads.

Enough daylight remains to get us down the last few miles of the trail, but we have time the next day, and my knee threatens mutiny. We unload, pitch camp, bathe in the frigid river, sun ourselves beside the waterfall. I make some half-hearted sketches in my notebook, too contented to take the work seriously.

We dine on the smoked shrimp that we have saved, as is our custom, for just such an occasion.

There is freeze-dried Neapolitan ice cream for dessert. Freeze-dried ice cream is one of the utterly improbable marvels of technology, only slightly less unlikely than freeze-dried water. Every time I bite into one of the dry bars with the texture of styrofoam, I am freshly astonished that it tastes like anything at all, much less ice cream, which it does in alchemy with the saliva in my mouth, *creamy* ice cream, recognizably strawberry, vanilla, chocolate.

We are camped in a grove of towering white pines. Their canopies admit a soft, reverential light. At our feet the pines have dropped a carpet of soft needles. High above us a flock of honking geese heads south. The sun sets and the air instantly cools. Mist rises over the river. When it is nearly dark, we build a fire and study it, smoking cigars, until the logs are reduced to embers. Overhead, the stars come out, one here and there, and then dozens of them, and hundreds, and thousands. The Milky Way makes a proscenium of light. The river tumbles over granite ledges. Otherwise it is so quiet we can hear our hearts pump.

Finally it is too chilly to stay up any longer. The sleeping bag warms in an instant. I think how good I feel, and then it is morning.

We began in a fog and we end in one. When I go to the river with my constitutional cup of hot Tang, the water upriver from the falls is as still as a rock, and where it falls, seems to drape the ledge rather than to tumble over it. The water looks more molten than

liquid. The sun has risen, but its rays have not yet
reached through the tall pines to touch the river itself. In this light the water looks gunmetal gray, and
the mists hover over it like the smoke that hangs
above chimneys on windless winter mornings.

We are closer than we have been in days to
civilization. Indeed, the place makes a connection
with civilization longer than almost any other in
Minnesota. People have been awakening along this
riverbank, rubbing the mists out of their eyes, negotiating their morning business in a Babel of tongues,
for centuries now. Perhaps the ancient human lineage
of this place, as much as the serenity of the warm
river waters wafting into the crisp September air,
makes it seem so primeval. I would not be surprised
to see a woolly mammoth lumber down to the edge
of the channel and dip in its great head for a drink.

We break camp, shoulder our packs, and follow
the ancient footpath toward the lake. Most final
mornings on a trail begin in ambiguity. I am reluctant
to admit being so near the end of something good,
and yet emotionally the journey is over. The concentration of the trail has been broken and I begin to live
in the world beyond the wilderness, thinking of appointments to be kept, telephone calls to be made,
miles to be driven. But it is not so for me this morning. The beauty of the place has so consumed me that
it cannot be driven away even in the leave-taking.

I think, as I take my first stiff steps, not of what
lies ahead but of the certainty that one day soon I will
return. Despite the hardships and vexations of the

walk, what lingers with me this morning is the luxury of this place—the luxury of silence, of still waters,
of flowers, of space and time that I find, freely given,
every time I come. It is the harsh instruction of modern science, I remind myself, that human beings were
not the motive force behind creation, nor are we
necessarily its end point. We are here by the happenstance and charity of nature, and every fertile rain
that falls or fair wind that blows comes to us as a
gift, and every product of wind and rain and sunshine
is likewise a gift, to be returned ultimately to the
earth as a legacy or otherwise lost. The watchmaker
may have been blind and the gene may be selfish,
as Richard Dawkins has argued, but the result has
ever been a kind of philanthropy to which we are
beholden, and by the grace of which we are now and
forever bound.

Halfway down to the lake we cross a magnificent
beaver dam, an elegantly arcing construction perhaps
three hundred yards long, the biggest I have seen.
A wooden footbridge has been built as a shortcut
across the shallowest part of the pond behind it, but
the bridge, too, has been flooded. We are forced to
walk the rim of the dam itself, teetering, grabbing for
balance at the alders and pin cherries that have
sprouted along its bulwarks.

Three-quarters of the way down my right knee
begins to nag shrilly at every step, and by the time
we reach the DANGER: ROAD CROSSING sign at Old
Highway 61, a sign that sends us into giddy gales of

laughter, I am limping badly. John suggests that I wait at the highway while he goes for the car, but I am sometimes a dangerously stubborn man. I hobble on, every step of the last mile or two a stab of sharp pain. We finally reach the car and shed our packs. John walks to the edge of Lake Superior to make ceremonial contact with its waters, completing the journey. I wait at the car, unable to manage the final hundred yards. Twenty minutes later, on the way back to the Gunflint Trail, we begin to talk about where we will hike next.

One of these days I will have to learn to slow down, to adjust my expectations to the realities of middle age, to travel according to the dictates of my knees rather than my heart. But not yet, dear God, not just yet.

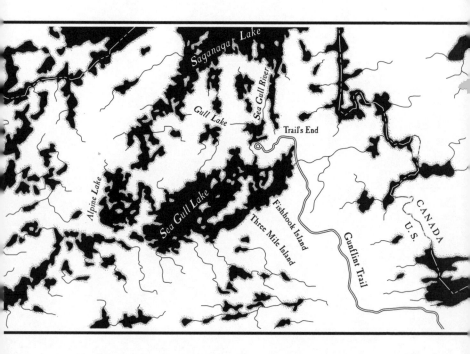

WINTER

By Light of the
Winter Moon

By Light
of the
Winter Moon

I spent one January reading
Henry David Thoreau's *Walden*
with three wonderful college
students. There was Nina,
broody and dark, who had
developed such an appe-
tite for the world that she
couldn't decide which part of
it to taste first; Verona, in
most ways Nina's oppo-
site, unfailingly sunny although something of a loner,
athletic, a biology major headed
toward a career in physical therapy; and
James, pale, thin, aesthetic, who played
the guitar, wrote songs and poetry, stargazed, and seemed
to regret the necessity
of living within a body.

We took the book a chapter a day, meeting every weekday morning for two or three hours of discussion of an intensity that only very bright young adults can sustain. They were drunk on the possibility of talking seriously with peers after years of having had to play dumb to get along in preppy high schools. They talked as though they were singing, for the sheer sound of it, sailing off into high philosophy the way a tenor tosses off high Cs. I had to take a nap after they left to recover my strength, and then I rushed off to the library to cram like mad until dark, breathing hard just to keep pace with them.

Near the end of our first week, someone in the group said, "You know, instead of just talking about Thoreau's experiment at Walden Pond, why don't we try it for ourselves? I mean we obviously can't go off one by one and build little cabins in the woods and settle in for a couple of years—we've only got three weeks left in this class—but we could find a cabin somewhere, couldn't we, and keep Thoreau's schedule for a few days?"

Two weeks later, we left for Wilderness Base Camp on Seagull Lake. The lake lies near the end of the Gunflint Trail, which runs from Lake Superior into the heart of the canoe country. In summer, adventurers by the score leave from there on trips into the wilderness, but the place felt as remote as a star that January night when we pulled up at the camp. We had driven for the last couple of hours in the narrow tunnel that the car's headlights made through the dense forest, each dip or crest or bend in the road presenting a new view that looked flat and unreal, like a black-and-white photograph shot in complete darkness with a powerful strobe. We traveled as in a spaceship across the colorless terrain of an alien planet.

I switched off the lights, turned off the engine, and we opened the car doors. The air was pleasantly cold and smelled of firs and pines. Our footsteps crunched in the snow when we got out and stretched our road-stiff limbs. One tiny yard light augmented the pale blue moonlight shining through thin clouds. The place seemed deserted. We had rented a cabin there for a few days—four rooms rather than Thoreau's one, wired for electricity but without plumbing, a place considerably more distant from society than Thoreau's cabin at Walden Pond if slightly more lavish in its appointments.

In a few minutes a young man arrived by ski from camp headquarters on the island just offshore, pulling a child's plastic sled loaded with canisters of drinking water. He pointed to a cache of sleds leaning against a supply shed. "Load your stuff onto those," he said, "and I'll show you where you're going to stay." We distributed the boxes of groceries, the bags of clothing, the backpacks of books and journals, our skis, and James's guitar among the sleds and, flash-lights in hand, headed up a hill and around a bend to a log cabin that looked straight out of *Hansel and Gretel.* After a quick tour of the two bedrooms, the common room with its space heater and gas-fired kitchen range, the little enclosed sleeping porch, the box beside the doorstoop that would serve as our refrigerator, and the path to the latrine, the staff member bid us a pleasant stay and was off.

I went down to put the car away. When I returned, the cabin smelled of scorched cloth. Nina had hung her damp blue jeans on the space heater to dry, not noticing its open flame, and had set them afire. Maybe coming here was a terrible idea, I thought.

Good idea or not, we had repaired to the woods. Now we would assume the pattern of Thoreau's days: up with the dawn, solitary intellectual work all morning, afternoons out of doors, a sociable evening meal, and then a return to our books or journals before retiring, pleasantly weary. We had each other's company, of course, but Thoreau entertained frequent visitors and walked—sometimes toting along his dirty laundry—to town almost every day, raiding his mother's pantry and catching up on the gossip. This fact has excited much disdain among Thoreau's critics. To think that he called the rest of us to higher lives when he himself behaved like a mere mortal! His mother washed his linens! Self-reliance indeed! Just like a male! Ours, whatever its merits, would be a reasonable, if brief, facsimile of Thoreau's life at Walden Pond.

The text for the next day was that perverse pair of chapters, "Baker's Farm" and "Higher Laws," in which Thoreau's customary good humor vanishes and he is at his preachy worst about Purity and

Chastity and other ideals of the new world order he is trying to imagine—without much success, even he admits. "The true harvest of my life is somewhat as intangible and indescribable," he says lamely, "as the tints of morning or evening. It is a little stardust caught, a segment of the rainbow which I have clutched." And, aware that he is being annoying, "Many an irksome noise, go a long way off, is heard as music, a proud sweet satire on the meaning of our lives." But what satire on the meanness of our lives—however proud or sweet or at whatever distance—is likely to be heard as music?

Thoreau claims to prophesy a life so gloriously transfigured as to be untranslatable into any language currently known, but when it comes down to specifics, he offers a mundane lecture on dietary practice. Avoid animal foods, coffee, tea, any eating that is sensuous rather than utilitarian, he advises. A few potatoes, some bread, a jug of pond water: these will suffice for the person who makes the body a temple. Make the body a temple, bring the life of the mind down into the body, Thoreau admonishes, but avoid all sensuality. I remembered that in one unintentionally hilarious passage of his journal, Thoreau upbraids God for having created a New England mushroom strongly resembling the human penis. But how does it honor the body to treat it as if it were not, after all, to its core a sensory organism? The body yearns and fights to make contact with the world and, indeed, cannot survive in any other way.

At Emerson's for dinner one evening, Thoreau

was asked which dish he preferred. "The nearest,"
he replied. Had I been Emerson, I would have passed
him a glass of tepid water and let him starve.

We ourselves devoured an enchilada casserole
laden with cheese and sour cream and jalapeños—
Verona's aunt's recipe—a big green salad, and enormous chocolate sundaes for dinner that night. We
retired feeling as uncorrupted as the snow that was
just beginning to fall.

The moon came over the ridge not long afterwards. I got up and went out to admire it. There
were veils of thin clouds with rents high in the dome
of the sky. The shrouded moon had a gossamer look
and gave off a blue-gray light, infusing everything
with its phosphorescence. The snow glittered. Just
above the forest hung the moon, as enormous as a
harvest moon. It seemed almost touchable, its close-
ness projecting everything else into the vastness
of space. I felt as if I were inside the crystal globe, in
which flakes of snow fluttered when you shook it,
that my grandmother kept on her dining room bu-
reau. Later, abed, the intensity of the moonlight in
my eyes awakened me. The moonbeams cast the
casement of the window at the foot of the bed onto
my chest, as if to hold me captive.

The most beautiful light in the world is the light of
the full moon on snow. Its glow seems to emanate
not from the heavens but from within the earth and
to radiate out into the darkness of space. The second

most beautiful light in the world is the light of the
midday sun on snow, light at its most transparent.
The difference between winter sunlight and summer
sunlight is like the difference between mountain
stream water and prairie river water, a matter of clar-
ity. Sunlight on snow sparkles; moonlight shimmers
on it. Winter days are naked; winter nights are veiled
in blue lace and sequins.

Thoreau's asceticism was not merely theoretical.
He was celibate in temperament as well as practice,
but even the solitary world—perhaps especially to a
saint—is an undeniably lusty place.

In the morning it was dusky, almost sultry, and occa-
sional flurries of snow fell. I sat at the little table on
the sleeping porch with a mug of hot tea, writing and
preparing for the day's discussion. It was a cozy place
to be on a dark morning. The hushed diligence with
which the students went about their studies, James
and Verona at opposite ends of the dining table, Nina
spread out on the couch in front of the space heater,
inspired my own efforts. I hadn't worked with such
concentration in a long time.

After lunch, James announced that he was not
feeling well and thought he would stay in for the afternoon. He slumped off to his bedroom and closed
the door. The rest of us got on our skis and glided out
to explore the lake.

Seagull Lake proved to be a maze of islands and
narrow, hidden passageways, one of those lakes it

would be a challenge to negotiate in a canoe. In three or four places we encountered open water among the islands we skirted. It would be dangerous to forget in winter, as one can in summer, that the canoe country is one vast, if intricately sculpted, sheet of relentlessly flowing water.

A burst of sunshine lasted four or five minutes. A flurry of snow, wet as kisses, fell, intense but lasting no longer than the sun. Gusts of wind swirled up and died away. The clouds made tableaux in the sky, like models on a runway. Now and then a shaft of sunlight streamed through a temporary opening in the swirling firmament, casting a spotlight on some tall and random pine. The ice cracked here and groaned there as we swept across it on our skis, the wind rushing against our faces. The whole world was awake and in motion.

Following a snowmobile trail, we passed the outlet of the Seagull River and beyond it a stretch of shoreline that had recently burned, as naked and pebbled as the carcass of a defeathered goose. Beyond that we left the beaten track and wended southeastward among islands shaped like scattered pieces of a gigantic jigsaw puzzle, avoiding the narrowest channels, which tended to be open or to have soft ice, until we came to a palisade, a sheer, eighty-foot bulkhead of pink and gray granite jutting out into the lake at a sharp angle like the prow of a big ship. Around the backside of the palisade we found a place where we could kick off our skis and scramble ashore. We climbed to the top of the cliff simply because, like a mountain, it was there. When we reached the shore again, the long shadows of late afternoon already stretched across the snowscape. Because darkness gathers quickly in winter, we set out at a more determined pace, taking the somewhat longer route along the edge of the lake so as not to risk losing our way.

We followed our shadows home beneath a clearing sky that gradually took on the mauve wash of sunset, delighting in the warmth and grace of the long, steady strokes of our skis. There is the same sort of pleasure in such measured labor as in dancing. Our ski poles softly tapped the crusted snow, playing upon it as upon a drum. As we danced across the ice, I took stock of this landscape, which I was encountering in winter for the first time.

I was struck by the silence of it, which, except for our own puny noises and the sigh of the air moving through the conifers, was nearly absolute. Early that morning, as I walked in the forest near the cabin, a raven suddenly uttered a ragged cry, as if even it were hoarse from the labor of keeping quiet. My skin had prickled at the sound of it.

Except for the rodent trails I saw when we climbed the palisade, we had encountered in several hours of wandering fewer than a dozen birds, three squirrels, and a few mammal tracks. Many critters present in a wild landscape, of course, scatter or hide at the approach of humans and others, given that it was winter, had flown south, or retreated to dens, or gone into hibernation. Still it was remarkable how vacant the landscape seemed.

And how extremely white, a dazzlingly pristine whiteness, even in its texture, which scarcely existed. The lake's surface had the sheen of a sheet of unexposed photo paper. I saw, where we crossed another skier's trail, the stain of his pee. In another circumstance, the mark would have been pallid and unremarkable; here it seemed so bold as to be violent.

But there was the moderation of the greens of the conifers and the grays and pinks of the stone. What would otherwise have been cold, forbidding, and stark appeared instead as gentle and forgiving, soft and beckoning. The mystique of the north is masculine, like that of the Wild West, but the northern landscape—unlike its western counterpart—is feminine, although hardly maternal, much more so in winter than in summer.

And the landscape conveyed a strange aura of intimacy. Vastness, emptiness, austerity have the paradoxical effect of opening up the self, of rendering it vulnerable to the persuasions of the heart. Noise, busyness, bustle, abundance—the trappings of industrial life—are enemies of intimacy. Is it any wonder that our industrial lives are so violent?

James, about whom I had been worried all afternoon, seemed much better when we returned from our excursion. He ate heartily at dinner, brought out his guitar afterward and performed for us, participated enthusiastically in the conversation, and went to bed late. Perhaps he was just tired, I thought, or had a touch of the flu.

At dawn the next morning I skied to the outlet of Seagull River to look for otter in the open water below a small rapids. There were otter tracks and gutters in the snow where they had slid on their bellies but the wary animals eluded me. I saw the trails of many small rodents, the tracks and droppings of a snow-shoe hare, three goldeneyes, and a pair of black ducks, and the rectangular excavation of a pileated woodpecker in the trunk of a white cedar. This was, after all, a living landscape. One simply had to know where to look for the life in it. Of course, this is true of any landscape, including the landscape of one's own body. Life is always and everywhere manifest in ways that eyes do not see nor ears hear. It lies hidden, waiting to be expressed in attentiveness.

I skied around the eastern side of Fishhook Island, halfway down the eastern shore of Three Mile Island, then back by way of the western shore of Fishhook. Most of the way my tracks were the only ones that I encountered, and I did not hear or see a single bird. In late afternoon I returned with Verona and Nina to the first rapids on the Seagull River. There, too, the birds were out of sight and sound, except for a downy woodpecker tapping a syncopated rhythm in the for-est. There were no new animal tracks along the river either, so nothing had moved through during the day, unless by water.

We made our way back to the cabin silently, each of us lost in private reverie. The landscape was so unadorned that it could be filled with thoughts alone.

In the night I listened to the clankings and moanings of the space heater, a sound I had almost forgotten. When I was a boy we spent winter evenings huddled around the space heater. Our house on the dark nights of January and February never quite got warm at the edges. If you sat close enough, you could put your feet up against the metal sides of the stove and toast them until they tingled with life again. The flames, giving off a blue and orange glow through the isinglass, were as soothing as a campfire. On Saturday nights, after baths taken in the galvanized tub in the kitchen, we sat in flannel pajamas at a card table in front of the stove, playing euchre and eating buttery popcorn. There was laughter in the house then. Later, abed in the loft next to the warm stovepipe, I would hear the stove pinging and popping in the living room below and feel that all was right with the world.

One noontime, though, I came home from school for lunch and found the yard full of neighbors and fire trucks. The stove pipe had filled with creosote, this had caught fire, and the red hot pipe had set the ceiling of my bedroom ablaze. The pipes were replaced with shiny new ones wrapped in asbestos paper where they passed through the ceiling of my room, and the hole in the ceiling was patched, but the smell of smoke lingered into the summer. As long as the smell of smoke lasted I had dreams of being trapped in flames. Every time the stove popped or pinged, I awakened, terrified. What kept me alive, I had learned, might also kill me.

The cabin's outhouse had a very high bench, too tall to pee into from a standing position, and a step to climb so that you could reach the seat. It seemed, when you were perched on it, outlandishly oversized, as if you were a toddler on a training seat. It was not, otherwise, an unpleasant facility. I grew up with out-houses and knew what to expect, but this was a new experience for the students. I expected them to moan about it. Nobody, however, uttered a word of com-plaint, not, I think, entirely out of reticence. Some of the inconveniences of primitive life have been greatly exaggerated.

We need a new word to mean the opposite of *nos-talgia*. If we are prone to falsely sweet remembrances of the past—the pinging of a space heater now evokes in me stronger memories of Saturday nights at the card table than of fiery nightmares—we are also sus-ceptible to the equally false notion that life before Cuisinarts and the World Wide Web was one of un-mitigated misery and hardship. The dangerous thing about this notion is the implication that Cuisinarts and the World Wide Web have something to do with happiness.

The smell of shit, to get down to the basics, is not the cruelest blow in life. It is possible to confront the reality of shit and still to be happy. This was one of the truths we had repaired to the north woods to remember.

The wind blew out of the south and the skies had been dark and threatening all day. When I went out for a few minutes at bedtime, I found a pitch-black sky and the temperature a balmy twenty-four degrees. A dramatic change in the weather seemed in the offing. Is it possible to become snowbound, I wondered, when you are already at the end of the road and determined to stay put?

My face had grown windburned, and when I arrived back at the cabin after my outing, the outer layer of my coat was soaked in sweat. I was healthy, contented, happy, and peaceful. I had time to think, the company of people I liked, lots of fresh air and physical labor, good plain food, and sleep. I could not remember why I thought, most of the time, that I wanted or needed anything more.

One big obstacle to a more deliberate and meditative way of life is that we are so easily bored. Boredom is the soul disease of the age. The more convenient life is, the more boring it grows. It is infinitely more interesting to raise a tomato than to buy one at the grocery, to concoct a sauce than to heat a ready-made one in the microwave, to negotiate a winding mountain road than to drive an interstate highway, to solve a mystery than to watch one on TV, to repair an engine than to browse through a pile of last year's

magazines while it is being repaired, to engage in a
witty conversation than to listen to a comic mono-
logue, to calculate the sum of a column of figures
than to enter the data into a calculator, to canoe
down a rapids than to ride the chute at an amusement park, to sail a boat than to be transported in
one, to travel to Brazil than to take a cyberspace tour
of it, to have sex than to watch a sex movie, to. . . .
The list might circle the planet.

The more bored we are, the more we feel the need
to be entertained. The more entertained we are, the
less interested we become in anything at all. Curiosity,
imagination, inventiveness expand with use, like
muscles, and atrophy with neglect.

I loved most about my students that they were
still in love with the world, still too unspoiled to
think that if they could manage to be bored, that
would be a sign of their superiority. There is, in fact,
nothing in the world more boring than someone
who is bored, unless it is someone who is bored and
feels the need to talk about it.

When I went out for my early morning ski the next
day, a gentle snow was falling. The air was mild and
the snowflakes fluttered to earth like billions of tiny
pin feathers. The light, beneath a featureless sky, was
gauzy and gray. The forest looked like a duotone print
rendered in shades of ash and faded khaki. Under
the new blanket of powdery snow, in which nothing
had been disturbed and nothing except the crystals
of snow moved, the forest seemed like something

out of prehistory, or like a place where time had suddenly been forced to an abrupt halt, as if the flakes were not snow crystals but bits of cinder drifting down from some faraway conflagration. Except for the sound, which seemed faintly to echo, of my skis making contact with the harder snowpack beneath the newfallen powder there was not even a whisper anywhere.

Then, as I came up through the deep forest to a ridgetop, a sudden gust of wind swept through the forest, and then another, and another. With each gust a powdery cloud billowed out of the branches of the trees and up from the forest floor, obscuring everything. Looking skyward, I saw that the tallest pines on the ridgetop swayed like reeds in a thunderstorm. Trees usually seem stolid and stationary, but in that wind they danced and gyrated, astoundingly graceful and supple. I stood between two weathers, the one at my feet, soft and soothing as a nursery, and the one a hundred feet up, as rowdy as a Saturday night dormitory bash. I would rather, I thought, have been at the party.

John Muir did once crash such a party. He climbed in a gale into the mast of a 120-foot Douglas spruce on a ridge in the Sierra Nevadas and rode the storm out, just to see what that would be like. "We all travel the Milky Way together," he reported, "trees and men; but it never occurred to me until this storm-day, while swinging in the wind, that trees are travelers, in the ordinary sense. They make many journeys, not extensive ones, it is true; but our own little journeys, away and back again, are only little more than tree-wavings—many of them not so much."

The aroma of balsam needles—a scent industrialists add to disinfectants to signify absolute cleanliness—is incredibly complex: sour and sweet, pungent and delicate, oily and dry. Perhaps, like the color white, it symbolizes purity because of its complexity. Thoreau assumed that purity is a simplification, but absolute simplicity is an elaboration, not a reduction, just as white is the presence of all colors and not, as one would think, their absence.

At bedtime the air was as calm as stone, the sky as clear as ice and studded with what seemed a million stars visible to the naked eye, the air was sharp and delicious—it tasted like mountain spring water—and the snow moaned underfoot. It was four degrees below zero, so quiet that even the silence seemed to sparkle—a stunningly beautiful night, perfect in every way. The balmy, cloudy days preceding it seemed now to have been cloying, heavy, and adulterated. The night shouted Hallelujah! The universe itself cried Hosanna!

We walked down to the lake, lay on our backs in the sumptuous snow, and gazed for a long time at the ravishing night sky. James, who had suddenly come to life in the out-of-doors for the first time during our stay, narrated a tour of the universe as it was visible from our snow beds, pointing out constellations, stars of distinctive brightness or color, the evidence of other galaxies. He fell silent and we watched and listened in the simple, awestruck way that people have been watching and listening for millennia.

Finally chilled, we got up and walked toward the yellow windows of our cabin, entered its steamy heat, made cups of hot chocolate, and read to each other from our journals, and when it was James's turn at the last, he read a poem about a fisherman who had caught a fish so vast that people in the village mistook its eye for the moon.

We talked the next day about education, and especially about the incomparable learning that takes place when the student's inquiry comes in response to a direct need and when the subject to be studied is present in reality rather than merely in the abstract. At Seagull Lake, the students read widely and wrote every day, not only because these tasks were expected of them but because the circumstances seemed to demand just such a response. When I asked, though, how this experience might be applied in the formal classroom, the students were stumped. If education is not the work of one's life, if it is not a constantly unfolding process, then there seems little prospect that it can happen at all. Nor can it happen, I think, in classrooms explicitly withdrawn from the world.

I taught a class one summer in a windowless inner-city elementary school. At the demand of the custodial staff, we were forbidden to post the children's work on the walls. Our discussions were constantly interrupted by pointless announcements blaring from a speaker in the ceiling. The principal talked about himself in the third person. One morning a little girl arrived at class in tears. Her bicycle had been stolen, she said. I took her to the principal's office to ask what might be done about it. "Well, Mr. Johnson is very sorry," the principal said, leaning back in his tall chair, his eyes fixed on the wall above the child, "but there is nothing Mr. Johnson can do about it, is there?" I thought I was in an insane asylum.

There was nothing to be done but to get those children out of that place. We went to the zoo. The children were incensed at the sight of the gorilla in its bare concrete cage. I had not anticipated this response. We talked at some length about it, did some research about zoos and gorillas, arranged to meet with the director of the zoo so that the children could express their outrage, wrote letters to the local newspapers and to legislators, created a leaflet to hand out to zoo visitors. Not long afterward, the zoo announced a major campaign to create more humane facilities for its animals. Perhaps the children had had something to do with that. In any case, they were heartened by the work they had done.

I was heartened, too. I had not known until then how intelligent and energetic and purposeful even quite young children can be at school, given half the chance. But I was also ashamed. I had not brought the same passion and energy to my own work; I had drawn back from the obvious next connection, which was that the children themselves were captives for most of their waking hours in a concrete zoo. I ought, after their example, to have been pounding on the principal's door and demanding to speak in their behalf. I ought to have been standing in the schoolyard handing out insurrectionist leaflets to parents.

Yellow light poured from the windows of the cabin at night, reflecting, perhaps, the golden hues of the wood paneling. It was a warm, beckoning, and nostalgic light: no such light is to be found anywhere in any modern city.

There were no light fixtures in our cabin, only bare bulbs in plain white porcelain sockets. How natural, attractive, and effective they seemed, and yet in a city house they would have been a mark of poverty and squalor. The same for the mismatched wall paneling, the bare wooden floors with the peeling varnish, the mismatched assortment of cast-off and threadbare furniture, the battered pots and pans in the kitchen cupboards, the miscellaneous tableware.

I thought of the eagle's nest I had seen that afternoon high in a red pine, made not just of twigs and sticks but out of whole branches and what might pass for small logs. It encircled the pine, sheltered from above by the tuft of canopy at the very top of the tree, which looked sufficient to keep out at least moderate rains and snows, and affording a splendid view of all the surrounding countryside. It met all the requirements of a luxury penthouse, save a kitchen, which an eagle would hardly want.

I couldn't think, sitting in the cabin, my own nest, late at night in the yellow light, of one more material thing that I wanted or needed. The place seemed perfect to me as it was. I couldn't remember, I realized, the last time I had had such a feeling.

How innocent that landscape seemed! I'm sure that if one settled there, it would prove far less remote from the blemishes and tribulations of ordinary twentieth-century life than it seemed to us as tourists. Still, in the silence of forests, in the austerity of cold, beyond reach of the marketplace, there does seem an innocence of spirit capable of transcending the ordinary pettinesses of life. It is, I suppose, the sort of innocence that could induce childishness as easily as purity—the childishness of simply not knowing—but that is not the inherent or inevitable result. Innocence need not be ignorance; it can also be a kind of courage—the determination to believe in the possibility of good despite the manifest presence of evil everywhere. To believe in goodness is the first step toward making it possible.

It was clear and much colder the next morning— fourteen degrees below zero when I first went out— and the ice on the lake was booming and cracking in protest. The sound was like distant thunder, but ominously present. When I went out on snowshoes later in the day, I saw in many places the cracks that resulted. They were very long, shaped like bolts of lightning, and no more than an eighth of an inch wide, unprepossessing for all the squalling of their birth. Thoreau marveled at the same phenomenon: "The pond began to boom about an hour after sunrise," he writes in *Walden*, "when it felt the influence of the sun's rays slanted upon it from over the hills; it stretched itself and yawned like a waking man with a gradually increasing tumult, which was kept up three or four hours. . . . Who would have suspected so large and cold and thick-skinned a thing to be so sensitive?"

I looked up from my papers and saw a pine grosbeak at the bird feeder just beyond the window. His head and back were a beautiful smoky red, a color for which we have, I think, no name, one that shows up often in the folk art of northern Europe. It is exactly right for these khaki forests.

I thought of all the color in this landscape: spruce green; the light yellowish green of reindeer moss; white snow; the cream color of mature birches, the russets and siennas of young birches; pink, green, and gray rock; black and orange lichens; the formal black-and-white attire of chickadees and downy woodpeckers; the bottle green of common goldeneyes; the scarlet of woodpeckers and the darker red of dogwoods; the pale blue of the sky; the yellow of the cabin windows in the night. What at first seemed a monochromatic landscape, proved on closer examination to be exquisitely splashed with color.

Every landscape has its season of extraordinary color. On the prairies of my youth that season is late autumn when the grasses have turned, a palette of browns, tans, bronzes, and dusky burgundies, the colors of a medieval tapestry, which glisten like shards of metal against the cobalt blue of the pot-holes in the long, low light of the late afternoon sun. In the Big Woods, where I now live, that season is early spring, when the forest floor is dappled with the lacy greenery of ephemerals bearing white and pale lavender blossoms and the meadows are crimson with the bark of dogwoods and the hillsides are banded in the pastel greens of nascent leaves, first the gray-green willows, then higher up the yellow-green ashes and ironwoods, then higher still the mint green maples and basswoods, and standing out against these greens, the dark, craggy, still-sculptural forms of the oaks, hulking giants, their limbs yet akimbo in winter slumber. In the north woods, I learned, that season of sublime color occurs in high winter, all the more enchanting because it is so improbable.

The silence was so deep that you could hear the wings of the birds beating against the air. Ravens squeaked through the forest as if their wing joints were rusty. The common goldeneyes sounded like little helicopters, the chickadees flitting among the cedars like scraps of fabric snapping in the wind.

I went out, for the first time in my life, on snow-shoes. My gait was slightly pigeon-toed and shuffling. I felt like an old man negotiating a hospital corridor in oversized slippers. But I liked the way the snowshoes slowed me down. Even the pace of skiing had already come to seem a bit frenetic. The preoccupation of modern life has been with speed, as if that were inherently virtuous, but it seems from the perspective of these woods that the real challenge lies in contriving to move slowly enough to experience anything at all of the world.

It was thirteen degrees below zero and the stars were so bright in the onyx sky that their light—the moon had not yet risen—cast our shadows upon the snow when we walked across the lake that night to camp headquarters. The students were in an exuberant mood. Even James, who had decided at the last moment to come along, flung himself onto the lake and made a snow angel. We found the camp staff waiting for us in the cavernous kitchen. They had brewed a fresh pot of coffee. We fortified ourselves with steaming mugs of the industrial-strength brew and then headed across a footbridge to Dominion Island. The narrow footpath on the island led through dark forest and then suddenly opened on the lake.

There, on a ledge above the lake sat the sauna, a squat log building sheltered in a thicket of firs. Its furnace had an exterior door. One of the young men from the camp was feeding logs into it. The furnace flames roared. Down on the ice a young woman poked at a big square hole with a long-handled chopper to keep the water from freezing over. A well-trampled path led from the doorway of the sauna to the hole in the ice. James and I waited while the women entered the anteroom of the sauna and changed into their swimming suits. Nina poked her

head out the door. "Your turn, ready or not!" she
called.

James and I went in. The tiny room, its temperature barely above freezing, was lit by a single battery-
powered lantern. The absurdity of what we were
about to do struck me as we stripped off wool caps,
thick leather mittens, double-layered coats, insulated
boots, wool trousers and sweaters, long wool socks,
thermal underwear, the garments gathering in great
piles on the pine benches. I put on a pair of flimsy
cotton shorts, feeling more than naked, as if I had
shed not only my clothes but the outer layer of my
skin as well. This, I thought, is what an insect feels
after metamorphosis.

I arranged an extra pair of woolen socks on top of
my clothes. When we made the dash to the lake, we
had been warned, we would need to wear woolen
socks or the soles of our feet would freeze to the ice.
Then I removed my eyeglasses, my last connection
with the known world, tucked them into one of my
boots so they wouldn't get broken, and entered the
steamy heat of the sauna. It hit me like a punch in
the nose.

For a moment, I was completely disoriented.
Then my eyes adjusted to the faint glow coming from
the red-hot furnace, which had been fired up at
midafternoon in preparation for our visit. I saw that a
tier of cedar benches faced it. James dashed a cup of
water onto the box of stones atop the furnace. They
sizzled and spattered, and my vision of the room dissipated in steam. When the air had cleared again, I

climbed to the top bench and took a seat, my back against the wall. I could feel my face going flush. My whole body swelled like a fritter in hot oil and then suddenly relaxed. I felt as light-headed as if I had drunk several martinis.

My body began slowly to braise. It felt so insubstantial that I imagined I might thrust a meat thermometer harmlessly into my chest to follow the progress as I stewed. There wasn't much conversation. We were all sauna novices, not counting the toy saunas one finds in hotels, and a little anxious, I think, about how our bodies might react to such an assault. For a panicky moment, I remembered that I was at the age where men keel over while shoveling their sidewalks, dead of heart attacks.

My flesh was beginning to collect in puddles on the bench, or perhaps it was only the sweat that gushed out of my pores, when the door opened a crack. "Anybody ready for a jump into the lake?" the furnace tender asked. Pretending gallantry rather than fear, I encouraged the students to go first. Each of them returned with a triumphant bellow.

Sooner than I had hoped, it was my turn. I went out into the anteroom, my heart pounding, pulled on my socks, ran blindly down the snow ramp to the lake, paused at the edge of the ragged hole.

Once I was on an airplane when the oxygen masks dumped unceremoniously out of the overhead bins and dangled in front of us like rubber chickens. The intercom clicked on. "This is your captain speaking,"

a voice said. It quavered. "This is for real. Please put
your oxygen masks on. If you need help, a cabin at-
tendant will assist you." I realized that in thirty years
of flying I had never paid much attention to the in-
structions for putting an oxygen mask on, but I managed. The plane plunged downward. My stomach
climbed into my mouth. The cabin was as silent as
death. I prepared resolutely for the end. I had not
been feeling well and had decided to make the trip
only at the last moment. "Dammit," I thought, "just
my kind of luck." The thought amused me. I had no
impulse to confess my sins, say a prayer, catalog my
regrets. My only regret was that it seemed to be taking so long for the plane to fall. If this was the hour
of eternity, I just wished it would hurry up and get
there.

"You're going to get cold if you stand there too long,"
the woman tending the hole in the ice said.

I took a clumsy step off the edge and splashed into
the lake. It felt like a cool shower after a day in the
tropical sun, absolutely wonderful. The woman
reached out her hand and helped me up the stair that
hung from the edge of the ice hole. I ran back to the
sauna, whooping like a teenager on Saturday night.

The plane eventually stopped falling, leveled out, and
skimmed along a couple of thousand feet above the
surface of the earth. "A little problem with the back
door of the aircraft, there, ladies and gentlemen,"
the pilot said, sounding like a new man. "It came

unlatched. You can take your oxygen masks off now. We'll be landing in a few minutes, and we'll get a new aircraft when we're on the ground. In the meantime, relax and enjoy the rest of your flight." The stewards did a land-office business in alcoholic beverages for the next few minutes. I'm sure I'm not the only passenger who regretted, just slightly, that our adventure had ended so anticlimatically.

"Next time," Verona said, "We've got to go all the way, duck our heads." And so we did. That plunge was even better than the first one. So we took it again. And again. We lingered in the lake a bit longer each time. After the fourth plunge, I no longer had the strength to hold my eyelids up.

We went back to camp headquarters, showered, and drank big mugs of hot chocolate to give us the energy to go on to our own cabin. I must eventually have gone to bed, but I have no memory of that. I slept as soundly as the frogs buried in the mud at the bottom of the lake.

The next morning I awoke thinking of the complex integration of minds and bodies. The water in that hole was on the verge of freezing, but my fevered body, under the influence of my mind, working from the delusion that the average represents some kind of reality, registered it as only slightly cold. The experience was not in the least painful, not even shocking, as by all sense it ought to have been. The brain is seated in the body, and depends upon it, but the body also, perhaps more than we appreciate, answers to the brain. Not to have the body and the mind in some sort of balance is, literally, to be berserk, as is, for example, the intellectual living only in his head.

When we talked about it over lunch, we agreed that this is one of *Walden*'s subjects. It is about finding balance—between body and mind, between the individual and society, between wants and needs—through the mediation of nature.

After lunch, James returned to his sickbed. Nina and Verona snowshoed with me up the east side of Three Mile Island, across the central part of it over a high ridge and then down through an old beaver pond, no longer active. It was studded with the rotting stumps of aspens and birches, as forlorn as a ghost town, which it was. We passed through a thicket of young spruce trees. A spruce grouse huddled on a limb of one of them, silent as a ghost, only the brightness in its eyes betraying the life within. We crossed a rubble of glacial erratics, ghosts of earth history, and came out on the western shore, where the red pines grow. Along the way we saw weasel tracks, rabbit tracks, squirrel tracks, and, on the way home in the gathering darkness, the tracks of three wolves that had crisscrossed one of the bays in the cluster of islands to the west of Fishhook and Dominion Islands.

The tracks in the snow mingling with our own, the rubble left behind by the glaciers, the pattern that the trees made, the sparkle in the grouse's eyes, the ruins of the beaver colony: each of these told a story, if one had the language to read them, some of the stories hours or minutes old, some of them millennia, even eons, old; and all of them convergent on that January afternoon.

In reading these stories, we three figures on snowshoes gave to them a kind of life they could never have had in any other way. The human species is not unique in making stories, but it is unique, so far as we know, in bringing stories to life in the mind. Our capacity for transforming stories into consciousness is our gift to the universe. To the extent, therefore, that we are ignorant of the stories waiting to be told, or incapable by illiteracy of reading them, or agents for the destruction of stories not of our own making, we condemn ourselves to a world smaller, narrower, and poorer than it has the capacity to be.

As midnight approached back at the cabin, an owl hooted outside my window. It got no answer, at least that I could hear from my bed. The owl persisted in its calling. I began to feel lonely in its behalf. I got up, dressed, and went out to look for it. Perhaps I spooked it. I did not, at any rate, hear it again. I remembered, as I returned to bed, that in many cultures the hoot of an owl in the night is heard as the herald of death. The prospect of death, at that moment, did not alarm me. This would be, I thought, a good moment to die if it came to that. It seemed to me as reliable a test of happiness as any: to be in a place where one would be content to die.

Some of the pines of Three Mile Island are more than four hundred years old. Certain funguses thrive for centuries. West of here in this same wilderness,

I knew, there is a cedar that has survived for a thousand years. In the scheme of things vegetable, the paltry span of our own lives is made plain, I thought. It seems to be a general principle of life that when an organism reaches its potential growth, it begins to die.

My students, at the peak of their vigor, reminded me morning, noon, and night of my own downhill path. I lived vicariously in their vitality, feeling exuberantly young again in their company. But when I listened to them talk, I was also reminded of the heavy labor of walking in the rarefied atmosphere of late adolescence, and then I was only a little envious of them. They helped me to remember that the breathing is easier and that the views are longer and grander on the way down from a summit than on the way up.

Nina and Verona went out late the next afternoon for a sunset ski. James, as usual, was in bed. I knocked on his door. He invited me, in a feeble voice, to enter. He was lying, curled up like a fetus, facing the wall. He had draped a spare blanket over the window. The room was as dark as night. I felt his forehead. He did not seem to have a fever.

"What do you think is wrong?"

"I've probably caught a bug," he said. "Maybe I'm just a bit tired."

"Can you describe the symptoms?"

"Not really."

I thought I knew what was wrong with him. I thought he was intimidated by the wildness and by the two women, the one so athletic, the other so daring. I thought he was too timid to leave the cloister of his own body and enter into the world. I was annoyed, impatient. I wished he wouldn't be such a baby.

"Would you like me to take you to a doctor?"

"Where would we find a doctor?"

"I'm sure there's one at Grand Marais," I said. It would take us the better part of a day to go there and return, I thought bitterly. I was almost certain the trip was unnecessary, but there was a remote possibility that he really was physically ill, and I was responsible for him.

"No," he said, "I wouldn't want to put you to any trouble," as if his invalidism was no trouble. "I'll be fine."

"Are you sure? It would be no trouble," I said, lying.

He did not answer. Perhaps I had revealed the truth in my voice.

"You can always change your mind," I said.

I went out and closed the door. It was getting dark, and it was James's turn to cook dinner. I started the meal myself. It had been his turn to do the dishes the night before, and he had made such a bad job of it that the women had washed them again after he went to bed. He had certainly never cooked a meal before, and it was possible that he had never washed a dish either. But he loved the idea of self-reliance, as he loved all abstractions.

While the dinner—mostaccioli stuffed with

spinach and cheeses and baked in a marinara sauce—
cooked, I turned on the lights, read without being
able to concentrate, paced the tiny cabin. I didn't
know what to do about James. I would insist that we
go in search of a doctor if he wasn't better in the
morning, I decided. And the women, who had said
they were headed toward the palisade, ought to have
returned long ago. A heavy snow had started and out
in the open the wind was fierce and lethally cold. I
walked down to the lake several times, but there was
no sign of them. In daylight, there was little possibility of their getting lost. They simply had to follow the
main lakeshore, where there was a well-traveled
snowmobile trail, and I had sent a map and a compass with them just in case. But after dark. . . . And
there was open water in several places in that direction. They knew the danger spots. I had warned the
women about them before they set out. Still . . .

One student perhaps mysteriously dying in the
next room and two missing in a storm. Dinner burning in the oven. This was what Thoreau's little experiment had come to. Assuming the worst, I turned off
the oven, wrapped the pasta dish in aluminum foil,
knocked on James's door and told him I was going
out and, dressed in my warmest clothes and with
spares in a pack on my back, headed on skis toward
the palisades. The wind was so violent and the snow
so thick that I couldn't see the tips of my skis. The
flashlight I carried made a light about as conspicuous
in that great void as a flickering match. I knew that
what I was doing was futile and stupid, but I also

knew I would never live with myself if the women
were in trouble and I had done nothing.

Not a hundred yards out onto the lake, I all but
collided with Verona.

"Oh! Isn't it an amazingly wonderful night!" she
cried. She was caked from head to foot in snow and
her hair flew out from under her ear muff like a flag.

"It is," I said, "but where's Nina? I thought she
was with you."

"Oh she is," Verona said. "She's right behind me."

"You go on up and get warm," I said. "I'll wait
for her."

Verona was on the college's ski racing team but
Nina had skied maybe a dozen times in her life. I
waited, my anxiety rising by the second, for another
fifteen minutes, and then set out after her. I came
upon her perhaps a quarter of a mile up the lake, still
on her skis and still headed toward the cabin, obviously exhausted and, I could hear from her voice,
very frightened.

At dinner the women recounted, ostensibly for
James's benefit, in ever more dramatic language the
story of their heroic adventure through swirling snow,
through howling wind, through utter darkness into
the wilds of the north, and how, through grit, through
cunning, through force of will, they had returned
alive to tell of it. Their cheeks glowed from the bur-
nishments of wind and cold, their eyes flashed. James
seemed envious. I was grateful for that, at least.

Later, as we sipped hot chocolate around the
stove, I apologized for not having made clear the rule
that they must travel together on such outings. I had,

in fact, been perfectly clear about this, but I was so thankful that they were all safe and so infected with their delirious excitement that I had lost touch with my own righteous anger.

The next afternoon, when we set out to hunt for otters, James came along.

We had been told by the camp staff that our best chance of seeing otters was near the rapids in the channel between Seagull Lake and Gull Lake just to the north of it. We headed there bearing into a stiff northerly wind, our ski trails drifting in behind us almost as quickly as we made them. Moving against the wind was as arduous as climbing a mountain. We did not see the otters—we did not expect to, actually—but we did see tracks that could not have been more than thirty minutes old, since they had not yet drifted over, tracks so fresh, it seemed, that apparitions of the creatures who had made them still lingered in the air.

There are two ways to see something in the wild, I had told the students. One way is to settle in somewhere and to wait as quietly and unobtrusively as possible until you have disappeared into the landscape. If you are patient, the life that is present there will eventually appear. Wildness is not found but revealed. The other way is to go in search of something in particular, like an otter. You may never find the otter, but because you were looking for something in particular with all of the focus and concentration that takes, you will encounter something else, equally precious, that you did not know you were looking for.

In our own case, that afternoon, we found fear.
The ice on the river below the rapids was thin and
the banks on either side were steep and shrubby. We
negotiated the banks as best we could, but in one
place we were forced out onto the open ice. We went
single-file, proceeding cautiously, sticking as close to
land as possible, and made it to the rapids without
incident. On the way back, however, Nina, who had
lagged behind, suddenly gave out a cry.

The ice had given way beneath her right ski. She
had managed to keep her footing and to extract her
ski from the hole in the ice, but she was soaked to the
knee and emotionally shaken. Verona inched toward
her and, offering one of her own skis as support,
guided her onto solid ice. Then I broke through, and
then Nina again, before we reached the spot where we
could negotiate the banks of the river. All of us had
skis sticky with slush.

We stopped to scrape our skis and collect our
wits and then hurried back to the cabin. The place
seemed, when we reached it, quite unharmed, tropically warm and utterly tranquil. Nina was still visibly
shaken. Verona helped her out of her frozen boot,
and Nina went off to change into dry clothes. James
started a kettle of water for hot chocolate.

When Nina returned, James, revealing a domestic
side none of us had suspected, brought mugs of hot
chocolate to the dining table.

"We could have died out there," Nina said. Her
hands still trembled slightly.

"I don't think we were in any serious danger,
really," Verona said.

"Close enough for me," James said. "What do you think?" he said, turning to me.

"I think Nina's right," I said. "We could have died out there. It was extremely stupid of me to be so careless. I'm sorry."

They all looked glum. We drank our hot chocolates in silence.

"Look," I said. "I don't want to scare you away from wilderness. We were in no more danger this afternoon than we were when we drove through the city a week ago in rush-hour traffic. In fact, if the issue were random danger, we were undoubtedly a lot safer today than we were a week ago. Danger is an unavoidable part of life. The issue is not danger, but carelessness, the kind of carelessness that comes from a false sense of confidence.

"Remember how careful we were in approaching the rapids? Then we got careless. We assumed that because we got across the ice once, we knew what we were doing. That's when we got into trouble."

"It's the same on the streets of Chicago where I grew up," Nina said. "Ignorance and self-confidence— that's the lethal combination."

"You get an A for the course, Nina," I said.

I thought, the next morning as I took my early walk, of the insistent physicality of Thoreau's program for right living. More than any other intellectual I can think of, he requires that the well-lived life be active in the body as much as in the mind. Thinking, for him, is clearly the higher activity, the one to which he devoted his first hours, but he spent at least as much time walking every day as writing and reading, and in his sojourns lies all the material of his work.

Another striking thing about him is how much of his life, although it was one of deep contemplation, was concerned with exterior matters. His effort was to understand the world first, and through it perhaps himself, and not the reverse. This distinguishes him from other contemporaries as sharply as his physicality distinguishes him from other intellectuals. For a man who spent his life largely alone and who made the major work of his life the keeping of a journal, he did astonishingly little navel-gazing. I think there are not three direct assertions about his inner emotional life in all the two million words of his journals.

The wisdom of our own time would be that the man had to be repressing something. Undoubtedly he was. Don't we all have hidden selves? I once read an astonishingly stupid study in which a group of Thoreau scholars were given MMPIs, asked to complete them in Thoreau's stead, and then the results were sent to a psychologist, who evaluated his anonymous subject and concluded—what else?—that the individual was neurotic. But the overwhelming evidence is that Thoreau was an extraordinarily happy man, able to face anything, even death, with serenity.

"One world at a time," he said, on his deathbed, to a friend who inquired of him about the afterlife. If this is the voice of a neurotic, let us all cultivate our neuroses.

Our cabin faced north. How many things in this country pointed north: the river, the winds, the tops of the tallest trees, the limbs of the windblown trees, the thickest bark on the trees. North was the only direction. Americans have been preoccupied with the mystique of the west, but the north has also had its powerful pull on us. Even Thoreau, who idealized the west and declared that it was the only natural direction, traveled, on those occasions when he left Concord, mainly to the north.

The allure of the north, of the west, is the allure of elsewhere. I have seen calculations of the number of years of an average life that are spent asleep, of the years spent sightless because of the blinking of our eyelids. I would hate to see a calculation of the number of years of my own life that I have spent wishing I were elsewhere. I would like, I have learned, to discover how to live in one world at a time.

On the return to college from Seagull Lake, I said suddenly, because it had just occurred to me, to Nina, who was driving, "I think we're headed in the wrong direction." A wonderful look of horror flooded her face. She thought I meant the remark literally. In a way I did.

Thoreau challenges us to approach every day so wakeful that the freshness and novelty of it, no matter how familiar the physical setting, might be noticed and appreciated, drunk in. I have not discovered how to achieve such wakefulness. I suspect Thoreau had not discovered it either, given the emphasis he puts upon it. He read travel books voraciously, and it occurs to me that of his four major books—excepting the journals—three are accounts of travels beyond Concord and the fourth is an account of the move to Walden Pond; and that by far his longest trip—to Minnesota—was undertaken when he already knew, on some level, that he was dying. His journals by then had become overwhelmingly technical in nature. He kept, he said, two notebooks, one for facts and the other for poetry, and his hope was for the day when one of them would be unnecessary, when his facts would have blossomed into poetry, but that did not happen; the deeper he plunged into factuality, the farther he drifted from poetry.

The perfectly Thoreauvian life would mirror Thoreau's days at Walden: it would be chaste, unencumbered by obligations to others, free from the burdens of getting a living—a life lived at a little distance from society. This would not, I think, be a life worth living. Thoreau himself recognized its impracticality if not its undesirability. He called his retreat to the pond an experiment and, despite the abundant pleasure it obviously brought him, left it after two years and two months, saying he had other lives to lead. But he was never again so ecstatic or productive. Thoreau put the question in terms of purity, but the question really is, "What degree of impurity can a reasonably decent life tolerate?"

To live life *deliberately:* What a riddle Thoreau has given us!

At the end of the session, James went to Scotland and read the English poets, Nina to Italy to study philosophy after spending the summer as a camp guide at Seagull Lake, Verona to Taiwan to teach English and to California to be a ski instructor before taking up her graduate studies. I went home to my desk and got on with my life, like Thoreau's neighbors, in quiet desperation. I answered the accumulated mail, returned telephone calls, made dinner, and felt the familiar sense of drudgery returning.

Only years later did I realize that I had failed my own course. It was I who had imagined, despite what I had taught, that a life of wakefulness was possible only in a tranquil retreat to some wild and unsullied paradise. There was a wilderness in my study, and in my kitchen, and in my bedroom, I saw, if only I had the alertness to discern it. "There is more day to dawn," Thoreau said. "The sun is but a morning star." At long last, I began to feel the heat of its bright rising.

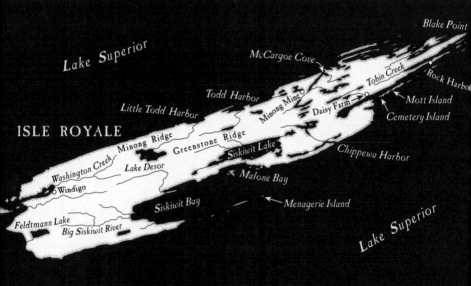

SPRING

Wild Isle

Wild Isle

I set out across Lake Superior one violent early June day, bound for Isle Royale, on the *Voyageur 2*, a solid, tubby sixty-five-foot boat without a single superfluous or luxurious detail. Also aboard were twenty-two Boy Scouts and their chaperones.

While we were still chugging out of the harbor at Grand Portage, Minnesota, the pilot's assistant came around to barricade the main cabin entrances with sheets of weathered and battered plywood. This maneuver was an ominous sign. Beyond Hat Point (there is a preoccupation with hats in the nomenclature of Lake Superior), the land quickly vanished. We entered a gray and disorienting land-scape, made up of the roar of wind, the whine of en-gines, the hard smacking of cabin-roof-high waves against deck and windows, the stench of diesel fuel, biting cold, and the constant bucking and twisting of the ship as it negotiated the relentless onslaught of whitecapped combers.

The leader of the scout troop trailed us in a fiber-glass fishing cruiser. For a time, we watched the tiny boat hypnotically, as if it were a bobber on a fishing line. Then we were able to see it only when it crested the waves. Then we could not see it at all.

We plowed on in a reverie of dizziness and nausea. After a few passes on a playground swing, I turn green. I popped a double dose of Dramamine, which made me light-headed and foggy, and hung onto the edge of my seat for dear life.

An hour into the journey, the first of the scouts, like the waves, began to heave. This had been antici-pated: buckets and bags for the purpose had been dis-creetly scattered about. Like corn popping, one boy went off, and then another, and then breakfasts flew everywhere into the clear plastic bags, which, for want of an alternative, the boys clutched in their fists. Only the smallest of them was unaffected. He wore his baseball hat backwards at a jaunty angle and danced about the cabin, ostentatiously munching on a fat ham and lettuce sandwich and calling out the contents of his fellows' breakfasts over the roar of the boat and the wind.

"Strawberries!" he shouted. "Blueberry waffles! Bacon and eggs!"

A huge wave smashed into the side of the boat. It lurched sideways, catapulting one of the boys across the cabin. The bone above his eyebrow caught the corner of a bench with a dull thud. He sat on the floor, dazed and bleeding, while the wound swelled. The boy seemed, however, not to be seriously injured and took the blow stoically. Slowly he turned the color of a Granny Smith apple. He had reached the level of misery beyond which there can be no perceptible increase. Curled up in a woolen blanket, he slept fitfully on a bench for the next four hours, stirring only to engage in another round of dry heaves, and another.

The captain of the ship, meanwhile, lay in the pilothouse bunk, an open copy of a paperback novel propped against his chest, dozing. His cabin boy was at the wheel.

When we finally came upon the western end of Isle Royale, stretched like a gnarled finger into the roiling cauldron, I saw that the pilot had arisen and taken the wheel again. Another hour, and we made the turn into McCargoe Cove, a riverine sliver of water running between forested cliffs two-thirds of the way up the northern coast of the island. The waters instantly calmed. The pilot's assistant came around, removed the doorway hatches, and readied the anchor ropes. We stumbled out onto the decks to watch the ship dock.

The sun glinted on the slab of open rock that

slopes up there into the forest. I got off the boat, shouldered my pack, climbed up the rock, and claimed a shelter from which I could barely glimpse the sparkling sliver of water on which we had floated in. A robin, that most domestic of birds, sang in a birch.

I laid out my bed, cooked supper, smoked a cigar, sipped tea. Perhaps I had always lived there. Perhaps there had never been any wind, or boat, or heaving lake. Down at the dock the green boy with the swollen eye, flesh colored again, fished cheerfully for whatever might come along.

So, in my own way, did I.

In preparation for the trip, I had been reading about the history of this place. Isle Royale, I learned, is actually an archipelago of more than two hundred islands, a constellation of ridges running northeast-southwest in the northeastern corner of Lake Superior. The ridges are the edges of sheets of lava extruded beginning about 1.2 billion years ago, when the earth's crust in the vicinity of Lake Superior cracked. The lava eventually spread over thousands of square miles, accumulating to a depth of more than ten thousand feet. It grew so heavy that it sank, creating the huge basin that Lake Superior now occupies. Rivers and streams, spilling over the rim of this basin, deposited sand, silt, and gravel across its bottom plain. Hundreds of times, the process repeated itself: a layer of lava, then one of sediment.

Millenia passed. The deposits hardened into sedimentary rock. More millenia passed. New cracks appeared in what was now the Lake Superior basin, thrusting the land that forms Isle Royale upward and exposing it in layers. More millenia passed. Erosion wore away the softer sedimentary rock, creating valleys and exposing the harder layers of basalt as ridges, steep on their northwest-facing exposures, more gently sloping on their southeastern faces, which slant away from the fault along the north side of the islands and toward the center of the basin.

More millenia passed. Glaciers descended from the north, grinding across the exposed surfaces of the islands and adding their own erosive touches, including more than seventy interior lakes, some with their own islands, so that it is now possible, by paddling across Siskiwit Lake to Ryan Island, to claim to have visited the largest island in the largest lake on the largest island in the largest freshwater lake in the world, for whatever that is worth. (It is, actually, worth something: Siskiwit is a big lake in itself, covering more than seven square miles, 142 feet deep at its maximum, and can boast its own species of fish—the Siskiwit Lake Cisco. And Lake Superior stores ten percent of the world's surface fresh water.)

The last period of glaciation ended only about ten thousand years ago, a blink of the eye in geologic time. In its aftermath, the level of Lake Superior has receded (it is now a bit above six hundred feet above sea level) and the land mass that includes the islands has continued to rise at the rate of about a foot a century. The prospect remains of further islands in the

Isle Royale archipelego, floating up imperceptibly over time into the morning fog.

The topographical result is a narrowly corrugated island landscape, its ridgetops high, dry, and rocky, its linear valleys boggy and, in summer, dimly lit. Although only forty-five miles long and, on average, about three miles wide, the main island feels much vaster. The trails mainly follow the ridgetops. The highest of these is Greenstone Ridge. Its summit is Ishpeming Point, elevation 1,377 feet, nearly 800 feet above lake level. Atop the point you get a splendid view of the surrounding trees and no sense at all of insularity. From a similar prominence on the Great Plains, you could see halfway to China.

The alternative to walking the ridges is to ply the islands and inland lakes by canoe or kayak. By doing so, you get an accurate sense of this as a world of rock and water, but little notion of its silent green heart—its chains of beaver ponds, its tea-colored bogs, its cedar swamps silent as mausoleums—where the few wolves still prowl, and in the summer water plants grow in neotropical profusion, and damselflies dart, and painted turtles sun on logs, and orchids (thirty-two species of them) bloom profligately. You climb to a mountaintop and its domain spreads before you, an open book. But a place like Isle Royale covets its secrets.

The pleated topography of Isle Royale is further accentuated by pronounced zones of vegetation: white spruces and balsam firs near the water, aspens and birches up the slopes, open rock and grasses at the highest elevations. Blue, dark green, light green, maroon and black, light green, dark green, blue: the colors repeat themselves up and down the ridges, often with a border of lacy cedars at water's edge, where they have escaped the fires that have swept across the islands for as long as there has been timber to burn. Each of these bands has its own light: sparkling blue at the shorelines, gray among the conifers, soft yellow among the aspens, burning white at midday on the high rocks. Even the climate runs in stripes: cold on slopes facing the lake, hot on ridgetops, moderate in interior valleys. You can feel the lake long before you can see it. These changes in climate are not subtle. There are places where the differences are as sharp as a knife. You can stand with one arm in each kind of weather and your body on the boundary between.

There is no brief way to know a place even so small as this. Places can be claimed but never conquered, assayed but never fathomed, essayed but never explained. You can only make yourself present; watch earnestly, listen attentively, and in due time, perhaps, you will absorb something of the land. What you absorb will eventually change you. This change is the only real measure of a place.

I wish to avoid certain adjectives in writing about Isle Royale, words like beautiful, primeval, pristine, natural, wild. There is already enough ambiguity about such places. Certainly Isle Royale appears to be all of these things.

Is Isle Royale, for example, wild? The main island

was being worked for its copper more than four thousand years ago, the earliest known mine site in North America. For centuries, fishermen have been making camps on its shores. Ships have been sinking on its reefs for nearly as long. It has been logged. At Minong Mine near McCargoe Cove, where a British frigate hid during the War of 1812, one can still find iron scraps from the narrow gauge railroad that carried copper ore from the pits to the harbor late in the nineteenth century. There were once villages on Isle Royale, and enough children to support schools.

I have read that in the first half of this century, several resorts operated on the islands, which had regular passenger ship service on a line from Duluth to Thunder Bay, Ontario, just across the Canadian border. (The hull of the ship, the *America*, is still visible in four feet of water at the entrance to Washington Harbor, where it sank one stormy June night in 1928, having twice struck the same reef. The forty-eight passengers escaped with their lives, but the ship's cargo of fresh fruit was liberated and washed up on nearby shores for weeks afterwards. You can't miss the spot; an orange-and-white buoy marks it: WRECK, it says with commendable directness.)

A few people still maintain vacation cottages at the east end of the island. There is a working fishing camp on Belle Isle. The main island is veined with hiking and portage trails and dotted with campgrounds, nearly all of them equipped with enclosed pit toilets and many with sturdy sleeping shelters, each provisioned with a broom. There are park buildings, two stores, a motel, a restaurant, a sewage treatment system.

The automated beacons of the lighthouses flash day and night on the outlying shoals. On clear days from the northeastern shoreline and from the ridge-tops you can see the smokestacks of the factories at Thunder Bay. Industrial pollutants from them and from the smelters and smokestacks of the North American Rust Belt precipitate in the rains that fall on the islands. Chlorinated organic residues have been found in Siskiwit Lake, which has never been touched directly by industry or agriculture and which has been isolated above Lake Superior since the glaciers retreated.

One night as I surveyed the stars from a road alongside the sewer works at Windigo, the port at the western end of the island, where yachts and fishing boats dock to buy gasoline, a moose approached from one direction and a red fox from the other, and down the road a beaver noisily dragged a birch branch across the gravel toward water. Moose are abundant on the main island, beavers manage to survive almost everywhere, and foxes have be-come campground pests. Are they wild? Is this wilderness? Does it matter?

It does matter, Adolph Murie once emphatically ar-gued. Murie, who died in 1973, was an eminent field biologist in the employ of the National Park Service.

He studied the wolves of Mt. McKinley and the coyotes of Yellowstone and published reports about them in the 1940s that are now regarded as classics of American nature writing.

Even before Isle Royale officially became a park, the first plans were drawn for a system of trails on the main island, the same ones I have followed on my trips across it. Murie sharply protested these plans in 1935. Three arguments, he noted, were being advanced in favor of trails: that they would give park officials some control over human activity on the island, that they would facilitate fire protection, and that they would enhance the average visitor's experience by directing people efficiently to its points of special beauty or interest.

To the pragmatic consideration—fire control—Murie answered pragmatically. First, he said, there were then—with the exception of the old maple forest on the southwestern end of the island and of one or two remnant stands of white pine—no extant forests so magnificent as to merit special fire protection. And second, he pointed out, Isle Royale is a narrow island: surely, he argued, boats could provide quicker access than foot trails in the event of a fire. "We must," he wrote, "guard against permitting administrative perfection to destroy our main objectives."

To the other considerations he responded philosophically. The essential attributes of wilderness, Murie said, are space and "low human incidence." Every trail in a wilderness, he argued, not only encourages casual use, but, more importantly, becomes a boundary that reduces the total amount of wilderness space. The proposed Greenstone Ridge Trail, which has since been built, would, he said, effectively divide the island in half, making of it not one wilderness area, but two, each unit half as large as the original, and, at best, only half as functional as wilderness. In fact, he noted, the proposed network of trails would reduce the island to a gridiron pattern of spaces, no one of them large enough to be, by the standard of adequate space, a real wilderness.

Further, he argued, when you "coddle" wilderness visitors by building trails and shelters for them, you do not serve people who are genuinely interested in a wilderness experience. The sort of person who would consent to wander the trails the Park Service had in mind, he suggested, would be happier at a resort. The real wilderness traveler, Murie said, does not wish to be led passively anywhere, but seeks the pleasure and stimulation of unpremeditated discovery. "In this connection," he wrote, "I recall a statement from Emerson which I quote roughly from memory: 'Go expressly to enjoy the moon and it turns to tinsel, but discover it on a necessary journey and its beauty bathes the soul.'"

This may sound elitist, but to read Murie in that way would be to misunderstand him. Murie's point is that wilderness is, as much as anything, an idea: the idea, ever more difficult to achieve, is of a place unaltered for the convenience of humans, existing solely for its own sake and entirely on its own terms. By this definition, Isle Royale long ago ceased to be wilderness. There may, in fact, be no such thing any longer anywhere in the United States outside of Alaska.

"In Wildness is the preservation of the World," Thoreau said in his great essay on walking. This is, perhaps, his most famous remark, but it is often misquoted: in *wilderness,* he is thought to have said, is the preservation of the world. There is an important difference between wildness and wilderness. Wildness is a condition, a state of being, something concrete; wilderness is an abstraction. Wildness is primary; wilderness, derivative. There cannot be wilderness without wildness, but there can be wildness without wilderness; indeed, wildness is as rampant as air.

The popular notion is that Thoreau was some kind of escapist, his journey to Walden Pond amounting to a flight from home and civilization. But Thoreau was not running away from anything. He was running toward the wildness in his own nature, where he believed he might discover his greatest potential as a human being. "Life consists with wildness," he argued.

> The most alive is the wildest. Not yet subdued by man, its presence refreshes him. One who pressed forward incessantly and never rested from his labors, who grew fast and made infinite demands on life, would always find himself in a new country or wilderness, and surrounded by the raw material of life. He would be climbing over the prostrate stems of primitive forest-trees.

We humans share with other animals both the habits of domesticity and the instincts of wildness. Animals make homes, tend their young, gather food, play, and, at least on some rudimentary level, communicate with others of their kind. To presume that only humans have domestic lives, or that only animals which live in association with humans have been domesticated, is to imagine a divide that doesn't exist in nature.

By the same token, we humans retain vestiges of the wildness from which we emerged. We are born fearing darkness, loud noises, falling, snakes, all fears essential to the security of our ancestors who lived in trees. We emerge from the womb knowing how to suck, to cry, equipped with the instincts for survival and for reproduction. The same might be said for a turtle, a wolf, a muskrat.

"The Old Lizard," the novelist Frederick Manfred called the brain stem, that physical remnant of our reptilian past, the ancient core of our ample brains, which still has its vital and essentially wild functions, despite the mediating influence of the neocortex, the physical manifestation of our cultural evolution.

The past cannot be repeated, but that does not mean that it can be extirpated or ignored. The wildness in our own past has not vanished. It exists in the deep recesses of our memories, in the language of our genes, in certain features of our anatomy like the brain stem. However distant we may be from it, wildness remains an essential part of who we are. To ignore that part of our being, to repress its memory, to deny its expression is to live in a disintegrated self.

When the self disintegrates, so does the ability to see the world realistically. The paradox is that the person without a whole sense of the self inevitably becomes delusionally self-centered. At the extreme, in mental illness, all of a person's available energy is required to keep the pieces of the broken self together, leaving none for relationships with other living beings.

What is true for individuals is true for cultures, too. A symptom of the emotional illness of the American culture is that it is able to make so little room for wildness, that it is commonplace to assert that whatever is not preoccupied with humanity, whatever is not subverted to the service of humans or contrived for their amusement, is boring, irrelevant, or escapist. The delusion of the primacy of the human in all things defeats healthy culture as the delusion of the primacy of the self in all things undermines the health of individuals.

One important reason for preserving wilderness remnants like Isle Royale in a world ever more intensively exploited by burgeoning humanity is that such places remind us that human-centeredness is a delusion. They keep us quite literally sane.

The Ojibwa name Minong, by which Isle Royale was known until 1699, when the French rechristened it in honor of King Louis XIV, seems to have had many meanings: turtle, the high place, the place of blueberries, island, or floating island—from Thunder Cape on the Ontario shore it does appear to float on the horizon like an apparition—but the word also means copper.

Copper was discovered at Isle Royale so long ago that the event has been forgotten. The earliest visitors to the islands are now known by the metal; they were members of what archeologists call the Copper Culture; what they called themselves we do not know. Later came the Hopewellians, named for artifacts fashioned from Lake Superior copper and found in the Hopewell burial mounds of southern Ohio. Later still, there were the Woodland Indians, whose copper artifacts have been discovered in Minnesota, Michigan, and Wisconsin. The Ojibwas followed. After them came the French, beginning, probably, with Etienne Brule in 1618, who collected samples of copper ore on his visit.

French explorers, on an excursion to Lake Superior from 1660 to 1663, confirmed Brule's finding, and soon knowledge of Minong's riches had reached the history books. Pierre Boucher, in his *History of Canada* of 1664 (the island was still claimed then by the British), reported the testimony of traders "that they saw an ingot of pure Copper, weighing according to their estimate more than eight hundred pounds, which lay along the shore; they say that the savages passing by, make a fire above this, after which they cut off pieces with their axes; one of the traders tried to do the same, and broke his hatchet in pieces."

By 1710, these copper deposits were fabled. "They claim," the intendant of New France wrote home, "that the island Minong and small islets in the lake are entirely of copper." Tradition has it, without any documentary evidence, that Benjamin Franklin, knowing of such reports, insisted on retaining Isle Royale for the United States during the Paris treaty talks of 1783.

Still, modern mining didn't begin on the islands until 1844, spurred by the demands of the Civil War. There were three efforts at it, the first lasting until 1855, the second from 1871 to 1873, and the third from 1889 to 1896. Although a single nugget of ore weighing 5,720 pounds was found on the island and displayed at the centennial exhibition of 1876 in Philadelphia, and even larger finds were later unearthed, the total production of copper proved rather small, and the ore itself was generally uncommercial, low grade. By the turn into the twentieth century, visions of a wealth of copper on Isle Royale had dissipated.

The oldest mining site on Isle Royale, and the largest, is just up the Minong Ridge from McCargoe Cove. I went to look at it. A pleasant, watery basin lies there, ringed by low basaltic hills. It appears to have been a young bog before the commerical mines of the nineteenth century altered the hydrology of the place. Now the wetland is divided by the high bed of the railway, which has become a footpath for the local animals. At its edges, the heaps of tailings are overgrown with willows and shrubs, but there are still places where the shattered rocks, in piles twenty feet high, remain barren of all but lichens and, on their summits, of young pines. Scattered among the shards lie hand-sized rocks bearing the green tarnish of oxidized copper.

The shafts and pits from which the main lodes of ore were extracted are tucked into the hills among trees that have gained stature for decades now. The narrow pits brim with dark brown water in which luxuriant growths of emerald green algae thrive and the trunks of fallen trees rot. I tossed a rock into one and it sank without a sound. The biggest of the shafts descends sharply into the face of a rock wall. A rusted bucket disintegrates nearby. The remnant rail line juts rakishly from its mouth, which has been blackened by decades of dripping water. I could see only a few feet into it. The sound of my voice, of dripping water, of my boots on the loose talus, echoed through it.

There was something sinister, or sacred, about those echoes, and about the mysteriously dark and deep excavations from which the ore had come. The mine has the feeling of a cemetery: the burial ground of lost dreams of wealth.

The early Frenchmen who quizzed Objibwa locals about the riches of Isle Royale were met with stony silence. The ore was sacred to the natives and used only in the manufacture of sacred objects, and they did not talk about what was sanctified. Perhaps it is their worshipful silence, which would seem to have been the right idea, that caused me to tiptoe through the Minong Mine.

On the southern side of Isle Royale, not far from Mott Island, which has become the National Park

Service headquarters, lies Cemetery Island, unmarked
on the standard maps. The story is that the men
buried there were laborers working the Ransom Mine
near what is now Daisy Farm Campground, that they
came into possession of a shipment of liquor, and
under its influence set upon each other in a fight to
the death. Hard-luck men doing hard labor for paltry
wages in an isolated setting far from home, from civilization, from women, thrust upon each other in
close quarters day after day until irritants smoldered
into resentments and resentments burst into flaming
hatreds. This is where such circumstances lead: not
to sacred, but to ignominious silence—the silence
of these men, heaps of bones now, scraped clean by
beetles and bacteria, mouldering in anonymous
graves on an uncharted isle.

Some of the Isle Royale names were bestowed by fishermen, many of them Scandinavians whose fathers
and grandfathers and great-grandfathers before them
had once fished the North Atlantic, people who took
up their work as a birthright.

They didn't earn much money at it. The fishermen
and their families came to Isle Royale every season on
the *America*, the same ship that now languishes off
the shoals of Washington Harbor. The *America*, not
coincidentally, was owned by Booth Fisheries, the
only company, for many years, that bought the Isle
Royale catches. A fisherman, his freight, and his family could book passage to the islands on credit in the
springtime. During the summer, the earnings from his

catches, as determined by Booth Fisheries, would be
applied against his account. When the end of the season came, in a normal year, a man's account showed,
if he were lucky, a balance of zero. The fishermen
were indentured servants.

But on the way home in the fall, the table in the
America's dining room was set with linen napkins
and silverplate, and perhaps somebody would play
the piano or the music box in the lounge, and there
would be dancing. To the children, at least, it was
very grand. And for the men, there seemed no imag-
inable alternative. "My father used to say, 'All you get
out of this damn job is an empty belly and a wet ass,'
but absolutely nothing this side of heaven could keep
him away from it," Ingeborg Holte has written in a
charming memoir of her eighty-some summers on
Isle Royale, first as a fisherman's daughter and then
as a fisherman's wife.

The names those fishermen left behind are full of
dark wit. Holte recalls the origins of some of them.
There is, she notes, a little island south of Wright
Island in Malone Bay that is unprotected from the
winds and always, therefore, frigid, as an unfortunate
family who tried to settle it soon discovered. It is
called Shiverette. Farther south still are two treacher-
ous reefs where her father found the fishing productive. He called them *Doden* and *Domen:* Death and
Doom. There is, Holte says, Starvation Point near
Rock Harbor, where you couldn't catch a fish to save
your life. And Checker Point, where two fishermen
were in the habit of vying, as if it were a game, for the

best sets. And the reef called Gilbertson's Farm, because it reliably yielded a good haul for a fisherman of that name.

Isle Royale was, as Holte remembers it, touched by finery. Singer's Resort on Washington Island was furnished, she says, with antiques imported from all over the world. The lighthouse keeper's dwelling on Menagerie Island was three stories high, built of stone, and, she recalls, had a cement walk and an organ, which Al Malone would invite her to play when she visited. In the main lodge of the resort on Belle Isle, the enormous fireplace was decorated with semiprecious stones. It was said, she reports, that the place also had a golf course and a tennis court, rumors she apparently never had occasion to verify. Holte herself as a youngster cherished a pair of flour-sack underpants with the imprint of a girl in a sun-bonnet on them, but she was forbidden to brag about them, and her mother, abashed at their frivolity, insisted that they be dried indoors after the washing. These were not people to put on airs.

Except when they went calling upon their neighbors. Then everybody scrubbed in the washtub and got spiffed up in Sunday best. Holte recalls her father describing her mother ready to set out on one of these adventures as looking like a ship in full sail: long petticoated skirts, a flowered hat with mauve veil, a coat tightly fitted at the waist and with leg-of-mutton sleeves, kid gloves, patent leather slippers. She climbed into the family skiff like a queen. "The fact that the boat smelled of fish and there were a few fish scales here and there, seemed most unimportant to Mama," Holte says.

As for the rest, they are the ordinary memories of growing up anywhere in immigrant America. She remembers the Norwegian bachelors who lived together for decades until, one morning, one discovered, to his irreconcilable disgust, that the other was in the habit of boiling the breakfast eggs without first washing the shells; he moved to another house that day. She remembers the family who kept a milk cow that had to be ferried from island to island in a boat to forage for food, and which, sometimes finding the transportation too slow, would leap overboard and swim ashore like a moose. She remembers what the Indians called the Fourth of July: "White man's big rainy Sunday," because that's how the holiday weather almost always broke. And she remembers the Fourth during the Prohibition when her brothers conspired to spike the Near Beer with moonshine. Late in the day a wind came up, and even the teetotalers were in no condition to pilot their boats home, so the whole party of celebrants spent the merry, stormy night on Caribou Island.

When Isle Royale became a national park in 1946, its inhabitants were given the choice of selling their property or taking life leases in it. Holte notes that it was the people who had lobbied hardest for the park, generally, who sold out. They couldn't live, she says, with the restrictions the park would have imposed.

But many of the fishermen chose the life leases. They had long ago earned advanced degrees in living with restrictions.

I walked from McCargoe Cove to Todd Harbor, arriving on a brilliant afternoon. Along the marshy path at the edge of the harbor dozens of garter snakes—the hardy species of the north country—sunned. Every few feet, one slid noiselessly into the grass for cover. Many of the animals on Isle Royale are furtive and seldom seen. Garter snakes are shy, which is regrettable because they are so handsome, but they are too numerous on the islands ever to be far from sight. They lead solitary lives in the summertime, but when winter threatens, they gather in great numbers—thousands, sometimes, in one place—and snuggle together through the cold months in underground chambers. In the springtime, they mate at the entrances to their dens and then venture off one by one to make their livings, sometimes traveling miles in search of a summer residence.

The island's frogs are also prospering. There are five species on Isle Royale, three of them so frequently encountered that the islands would seem naked without them. In the springtime the choruses of the spring peepers, which congregate at the beaver ponds and interior swamps to breed, make a constant, shimmering evening obligato, as evocative of the season as the sawing of crickets in August. In every little puddle along a hiking trail I encountered

the green frog, an elegant dark olive in color, a small
creature with a big voice that sounds like the pluck-
ing of a loose bass banjo string. In drier places I often
saw the wood frog, which looks and moves more like
a little toad than a frog and also has an astounding
voice—fortunately it does not carry far—something
between the quack of a duck and the whine of a chain
saw, a clear demonstration of the variability of sexual
appeal.

I approached a fire ring at the bend in the bay,
where there is a picnic landing for boaters. The ring
was blanketed in tiger swallowtail butterflies that had
come to partake of a party's leftovers. Swallowtails,
too, are characteristic of the mixed forests of the
north country, birches and willows being among their
favorite plants. They seem nearly as abundant as the
mosquitoes, and vastly more welcoming, their yellow
and black bodies flashing like flying flowers in every
grassy opening and sunny glade. A Danish legend
holds that butterflies are the souls of the dead, the
happiest vision of an afterlife that I know.

Every visitor to Isle Royale is also bound to notice
the abundance of ladybugs, almost the only bug generally regarded as endearing. According to Edwin Way
Teale, French peasants call them the "Cows of the
Lord," and in Sweden they are sometimes known as
"Virgin Mary's Golden Hens." Ladybugs have been
thought to bring almost every kind of blessing, from
good weather to good husbands to instant relief from
toothaches. I saw hosts of them on the rocks along

the Lake Superior shoreline as I made my way toward
my campsite, attracted, perhaps, by the rich debris of
tree pollen in the shallow shoreline waters.

I made a camp at the eastern tip of the harbor, a
fine ledge of rock shaded by tall pines and carpeted
in soft needles with a good view of the Ontario
shore and the setting sun. I had no sooner put down
my pack and begun the routine—so comforting to
trekkers—of setting up house when the sun disappeared. Looking up, I saw that the sky to the
north had turned the color of a bruise.

A violent storm seemed in the offing. I hurried
to get the tent up and dinner underway, hoping to be
ready to take refuge when the deluge came. Three or
four minutes later, a deep stillness fell over the land.
As suddenly, a fierce, cold wind began to howl in the
tops of the swirling pines. In a minute, the wind died,
the temperature warmed, and the skies took on the
dull gray look of an all-night rain. For about two
minutes a gentle rain did fall. Then abruptly the rain
stopped, and the skies turned blue again, the late-
afternoon sun casting lovely long shadows upon the
camp work. By the time the supper water was boiling,
there was a cool breeze again out of the north, where
scattered cirrus clouds drifted high on the horizon,
portending another storm.

I had just had a fine demonstration of the mercu-
rial moods of the Lake Superior weather, which make
crossing its waters such hazardous business and
account for the dozens of shipwrecks that ring these
islands.

One other thought gave me pause as I thought over soup and pasta about what I had seen: Not so long ago in the global scheme of things, these islands had been barren rock, and then places where only lichens survived. Slowly the lichens dessicated the rock, making niches in which less venturesome plants might root, and a flora emerged upon the islands. The flora now includes not only native species carried as seeds to the island by winds and water and swimming or flying creatures, but also dandelions, and mulleins, and plantains, European invaders carried there by humans. It also includes, at Daisy Farm, apple trees, which the flora lists describe as "escaped from cultivation." I love the image of apple trees striking out for freedom, like feral cats.

The fauna followed. Some of the creature settlers crossed the infrequent bridges of ice, some flew, some drifted in. But some of these creatures swam to the islands, testing the fickle skies, through waters that, even as I ate, measured only thirty-six degrees Fahrenheit and were not going to get much warmer. They were the heroes of exploration of this place, if any such idea as heroism makes sense among animals, and they had the luck of the ladybugs with them.

I went on to Little Todd Harbor. I sat along the shore there in the evening, sheltered from the chill breeze drifting off the lake. A brood of young red-breasted mergansers—sea ducks, the commonest on the

islands—came cheeping around the bend, reminding
me of the sound I used to hear as a boy at our rural
post office when the spring shipments of baby chickens had arrived. The young ducks were blithe and
oblivious. They cavorted to within a few feet of me.
Suddenly mama appeared, took one look at me, and
gave a single loud quack. The chicks instantly pirouetted in unison and scampered out of sight, moving
so fast they were half out of the water, their orange
feet churning. They were as swift as a school of fish.
I shook my head. Where, I wondered, had I gone
wrong as a parent? Perhaps, I thought, I ought to
take lessons in parenting from an old merganser.

There were eleven gray wolves on Isle Royale the
spring I visited; the spring before there had been
fourteen; once the island supported as many as fifty
wolves. Researchers have hypothesized that the pack
is gradually losing its genetic vitality. In the meantime, through the 1980s, the moose population
soared. Large moose populations have an impact on
the vegetation of the island. Their browsing favors
white spruce over balsam fir and reduces populations
of such plants as mountain ash, American yew, and
American devilsclub, a remarkable constituent of the
Isle Royale flora that occurs nowhere else east of the
Rocky Mountains. The latter shrub gets its name
from its fierce armament of sharp thorns. It is now
limited to Blake's Point at the eastern extremity of
the main island and to a few of the outlying islands.
The moose themselves suffer when their populations

soar: among the consequences are starvation and in-
festations of winter ticks (a single animal may harbor
thousands of them) that cause hair loss and subsequent death by exposure.

The wolf population at Isle Royale, first recorded
in 1951, has been the subject of intensive long-range
study, work enhanced by the population's confine-
ment to a small, insular, and isolated setting. A sci-
entific argument can be made for following their fate
to the bitter end. The introduction of wolves and
moose, while it represented a dramatic change in the
ecology of the islands, this argument would go, was a
natural occurrence, neither artificially induced nor
enhanced, and reflects, therefore, the dynamic nature
of a wild community, a dynamism that ought to be
honored.

A compelling argument can also be made for in-
tervening, if that proves necessary, to maintain the
wolf population on Isle Royale. Rolf Peterson, who
has been involved with the long-term study of wolves
on Isle Royale for twenty-five of its thirty-five years,
makes that argument in his book, *The Wolves of Isle
Royale: A Broken Balance.* Wolves, he notes, play a
vital role in the present ecology of Isle Royale. It is
their presence through the past forty years, he argues,
that has resulted in Isle Royale being the closest thing
we have in our national system of wilderness preserves to a self-sustaining ecosystem, a place that is
both "cathedral and laboratory. But of what use is
a cathedral without sacred imagery?" he asks. "Of
what value is a laboratory without subjects?" What

happens at Isle Royale may set an important precedent, Peterson argues. "If the wolves of Isle Royale are threatened by insularity, can the grizzlies of Yellowstone be far behind?" There may well come a time when Isle Royale has so changed that maintaining a wolf population there will make no sense. "But this time around," he says, "at the dawn of a new millenium, I must vote for the wolves."

Isle Royale offers a sharply drawn demonstration, in miniature, of the dilemmas and conflicting values that accompany the management of any wilderness area. Are our wilderness preserves museums or are they laboratories? How much should they be managed and to what end? Where should the line be drawn between benign neglect and the failure of stewardship?

The park seems an ideal place to ponder these questions. Because of its relatively harsh environmental setting, it offers an ecosystem that, while enormously complex, is nevertheless, relatively less so than than those in many other national parks. Though marred by air and waterborne pollutants, it is still relatively unspoiled. And because it is an island, the effects of human encroachment are comparatively easily managed: its animals are not going to wander onto nearby farmlands or infect neighboring stock with their diseases; its remoteness limits visitation; the Lake Superior shores nearest it are not likely to experience any substantial industrial

or residential growth; and the cold waters encircling
the island offer no opportunities for speculative development along its boundaries; for much of the year
the park is closed to humans. If the ideals of wilderness, whatever they are, cannot be preserved on Isle
Royale, it is unlikely that these ideals can be maintained anywhere.

One option no longer available is simply to leave
wilderness areas alone, to let them be whatever they
will become without human management. The
legacy of the industrial age is a world in which everything, even wildernesses, requires human management. My friend the agricultural economist snickers
sardonically when he says, "You know those farm animals aren't so dumb. For centuries, they served us,
and now they've finally turned the tables. These days
they live out their lives being waited upon hand and
foot by farmers. Pretty slick, I'd say." Just as we labor
from dawn until dusk to afford our labor-saving de-
vices, so we are now condemned to be nursemaids to
a natural world that is ailing because of our improve-
ments upon it.

We set out to make a world fashioned for our own
comfort and convenience, forgetting that we are as
much the products of biology as of our own ingenuity.
And so we made a world, from the perspective of nature, in which there are only islands, fragile on that
account and unpredictable, and we ourselves drift in
the increasingly barren seas among them, as through
a flooded junkyard, searching at random for the parts

with which to assemble a whole world again, one that runs on some power other than our own.

I walked from Little Todd Harbor to Lake Desor. One night while I was camped there, I heard the cry of a lone wolf far away. Sometimes that cry has sounded to me exuberant, sometimes mournful, and sometimes it has made the hair on the back of my neck rise, as the hair on the back of a wolf bristles when the animal is threatened. But that night the cry sounded to me defiant. "Yoooooou!" the wolf seemed to be saying, "Yooooooooou!" The accusation echoed through the narrow valley and across the waters of the lake, as through deserted city streets.

"Listen up," the wolf said. "Pay attention. I intend to survive. Do you?"

Isle Royale's moose population is currently immense. You can scarcely walk a hundred yards anywhere on the main island without encountering a pile of their scat. Every mudhole bears their tracks.

A moose looks like the discarded early draft of an idea for an animal. Encountering one, especially a bull, is like watching a paleontology exhibit come alive. Its gangling legs, its long humped nose, its big ears, its ungainly antlers, its swayed back, its apparently vacant stare: everything about it seems ridiculously miscalculated. "Ugly as sin," my grandmother would have said, in the days when people still took sin seriously.

Still, there is something compelling about a moose. Up close, its size always astonishes. Only two other land animals on this continent, grizzlies and bison, command a similar physical presence. In winter prime, its coat has a rich, chocolate sheen, as sleek as a mink's. It looks soft and silken. Seeing a moose, you get the wild impulse to run your fingers through its hair, to hug it.

When, from an island ridge, you see one in the valley below, standing, perhaps, in a beaver pond at midday to escape the heat and the insects, and it is unaware of your presence, or when you see one browsing water plants—for their salts, it is thought—along a northern shore in the early morning mist, the moose seems a lord of the land, as regally at home as a bear in a meadow or a horse on a grassy hilltop.

The animal looks—and is—dim enough to be dangerous. I chanced upon one on my way to Little Todd Harbor. It lumbered down the trail for half a mile, stopping every hundred yards to see if I were still behind it. It was like following a duck or a heron—something bird-brained—down a river.

Most big animals stalk the forest softly, but not a moose. It crashes this way and that, loudly snapping sticks and small branches. But when you search for the lummox a minute later, it has mysteriously vanished, its movements inaudible. How can something so lumbering conspire to be so instantly invisible? You know then that you have been watched, everywhere you have gone, at close range, by these creatures at

least six or seven times your size. You get the uncanny
feeling of being a mouse in a kingdom of elephants.

A couple of nights later, I was awakened by the
sound of a creature galumphing its way up a creek.
Splish! Splash! Splish! Splash! the animal went in a
loud, slow, strangely offbeat rhythm, sounding like
a break dancer on stilts working in water. The night
was dark and I couldn't have seen the animal anyway,
but I didn't need to see it to know what it was. Only
a moose could have created such a wacky ruckus.

Ingeborg Holte tells a story about an Isle Royale
moose that makes the adjective "elephantine" seem
appropriate in another way. I am thinking of the remarkable bond that apparently lingers among elephants even after one of them has died. The moose
confronted Holte one day at Little Greenstone Beach,
where she and her husband had gone to search for
gems. She had noticed it at the edge of the woods
when they had arrived by boat, a gaunt cow showing
the ravages of a hard winter—protruding hip bones,
fur missing in great patches. Holte thought nothing
of it, moose having been a regular part of her life
since she was an infant. She bent to the task at hand.

Suddenly she heard stones tumbling down the
beach and, looking up, saw the moose charging toward her, the hair on the nape of its neck raised, its
eyes rolling so that only the whites showed, its teeth
bared. As the creature neared, it reared on its hind
legs, its front legs flailing. Holte knew a single kick
might kill her.

She had no idea what she had done to enrage the
moose. She tried to cry out, to flee, but in her terror
she was voiceless and powerless to move. Holte's
husband, down the beach, had, just then, the premo-
nition to look in her direction. He flew to her rescue.
The moose could concentrate on only one of them
at a time. Between them, the Holtes were able suffi-
ciently to distract the animal so that they could both
scramble up a steep cliff to an old mining cave. She
took refuge inside; he stood watch at the entrance.

The moose knew where they were and all afternoon kept a close eye on them. It could have gotten
to the cave, but stood, instead, at water's edge, alternately staring up the cliff and pawing its hooves
against the beach pebbles in warning, uttering some
sort of soft entreaty over and over again out toward
the lake. Listening to it, the animal's captives began
to feel for it an inexplicable pity.

The long shadows of evening finally came, and
with them the mosquitoes. Holte's husband wanted
to make a try for the boat, but she was still too terrified to budge. He urged moving, at least, to a larger
cave where they might build a smoky fire as a defense
against the insects.

Then Holte saw—it may have been a revelation of
the new light—that the big boulder in the lake near
where the moose stood was made not of stone, but of
flesh. It was the body of the animal's calf. The baby
had probably wobbled out into the water, fallen,
and drowned. Holte had come, without knowing it,

between the calf and its mother, and the mother
could now forget neither the calf nor the intruders.

The Holtes began to dash to the larger cave.
Startled, the moose bolted to the edge of the woods.
Seeing their chance, they made a run across the
beach instead, reached the boat, and launched it
before the cow moose returned to the defense of her
baby, tracking the humans across the stones with
her nose, like a wolf.

In the night, the direction of the wind shifted.
The Holtes, thinking the shift might have carried the
body of the calf to its mother, returned the next day
to the beach. The body had drifted in, but nothing re-
mained of it except a few patches of hair. The wolves
had already scavenged it, and there was no sign anywhere of its mother.

I descended the Minong Ridge at the place where
it crosses one branch of the upper reaches of
Washington Creek and was just about to set my
right boot onto a stepping stone when a dark, lithe,
long-tailed animal slipped around an alder and disappeared into a thicket of shrubs. I had a second's
look at it, if that, before it had vanished. A cursory
exploration in the direction it had gone revealed no
evidence of a readable footprint.

Perhaps if I had not been so intent on getting to
Windigo before the store closed (I did not yet know
that it hadn't opened), if there had not been a boat to
meet in the morning, if I had not committed myself

to obligations that bound me to meeting it, perhaps
if I had ever learned to travel freely, or believed more
deeply in the opportunities the moment brings, I
might have unburdened myself of my pack and gone
in search of that fleeting image. But I didn't. I looked
where the creature had gone, replayed the image of it
in my eye, stepped to the opposite shore of the little
stream, and trudged uphill, beads of sweat gathering
in the small of my back, hoping that some less fleeting presence might appear along the way to compen-
sate for the loss.

I thought that it might have been an ermine in
dark summer coat, or a mink, or even an otter,
although it seemed small for that. Most likely, I
decided, the creature was a mink. Later that day,
I would claim to have seen a mink, and to have been
pleased at the sight of it, but it was the kind of lie
we tell when we are disappointed. The truth was,
I had seen a fleeting shadow for a brief moment, a
thin thread of experience, and had embroidered it
into a story. We tell stories like this all the time;
one's life consists of the sum of them.

I can see the moment even now, a long time later,
just as if it had freshly happened: the glance to the
left, where the tan water ran through the green stems
of a marsh marigold bright with golden flower, the
flurry of motion, the flash of visual data: long, lithe,
brown or black, with tail. It remains one of my most
vivid impressions of Isle Royale. I have stored it with
a hundred thousand other impressions just like it of a

thousand other places. I want to extract them, make them solid, and render them as something concrete: a collage, maybe, or a quilt.

See, I could then say, this is the essence of wildness; this is what we must not forget: how brief life is, how unexpected, how little of it we glimpse, how rapidly it changes.

I, like the next person, struggle to make sense of what I have seen and heard. I tell stories about wild places, as if I had discovered anything at all. If I told the truth, everything I described would be indistinct and on the run. This would be a true picture of the wild places I have known, including those of my own heart: I would be standing at the center of the frame, and at its edges one would see the tails of things, mysterious and alluring, their owners dashing for cover.

I was camped at Washington Creek, having packed there from Lake Desor at the end of a four-day trek from McCargoe Cove along the Minong Ridge. The walk from Lake Desor is eleven and a half miles, and the last two or three of them, with discouraging frequency, descend and climb, descend and climb. I felt good, sitting idly at the creek's edge, eating the last morsels of food from my pack.

I watched as a small log drifted past. It was an unremarkable event, and I thought nothing of it. A minute later, the log drifted past again, this time floating in the opposite direction, or so it seemed. I knew I was tired, but I hadn't thought I was at the point of hallucination. A couple of minutes later, the log sailed past a third time, headed properly downstream. I looked twice to be sure I was seeing what I thought I was seeing. Still, I was reluctant to admit it.

Then the log reversed course again. The conclusion was unavoidable. The creek was flowing both up and down stream, raising and lowering in level as it did. Now there was a long sandbar in front of me, and two minutes earlier there wasn't.

At the time, I was reading a little book called *The Life of Isle Royale.* By happenstance, I stumbled almost immediately upon an explanation: When streams empty into long, narrow harbors, as Washington Creek does, wind driving water upharbor meets the discharge of the creek and builds until the swell forces a reversal of flow. "Washington and Tobin Creeks and the Big Siskiwit River exhibit this phenomenon quite markedly," I read. "Over Lake Superior as a whole, differences in atmospheric pressure cause similar, though less regular, effects. Such oscillating waves, known as seiches, occur in many lakes, bays and gulfs of the world." So I had a name for the phenomenon—I was watching a seiche—and the name was strangely comforting, an assurance that what had looked so improbable was real and had been noticed before.

Names are not always so reassuring. Riding the ferry back from Isle Royale to Grand Portage the next day in blessedly calm weather, my old fear of open water nevertheless suddenly returned and I thought to investigate whether there was a lifeboat aboard.

I found one, a bright yellow dinghy, lashed to the roof of the main cabin. "Plastic Bouyancy Accessory," its label said in bold black letters. I tried to imagine the state of mind of the person who had devised it, to recreate the conversation that took place at the product development conference where it was first proposed, but my imagination failed me. I climbed down from the railing and reported to my shipmates that we were under the protection of a plastic bouyancy accessory. We were not the least comforted by the news.

Names can be both blessings and curses. On the one hand, they can be—perhaps inevitably are— reductive. A name stands for but does not describe a thing; approached casually or carelessly, the act of naming, therefore, quickly becomes a way of labeling, of categorizing, a substitute for knowing, and every system of categories drifts compulsively toward hierarchy.

On the other hand, it is impossible for me to imagine knowing something well—much less loving it—without needing to name it. A name is a form of acknowledgment—more than that, of embrace.

I encourage my students to learn the names of at least the common plants and animals around them. This is, I tell them, a way of establishing an intellectual and emotional as well as physical connection with the natural world. And, I say, it is a useful discipline. To learn the names of the trees on the campus or on your street is to notice that there are not just trees, but many kinds of them, each with distinctive qualities and character, a place of origin, a history, a strategy for survival. Naming trees is a way of learning to see them not merely as a type, but as individuals, which is the first step in appreciating diversity in life and its utility and beauty.

Sometimes I get vehement resistance. Isn't there, my students ask, a way of knowing that acknowledges difference—and the wonder of it—without resorting to names? Aren't the names themselves the first step in the demystification of nature?

I have to agree that it has often seemed so. In many cultures one does not name those things that are most sacred—as copper was once unnamed on Isle Royale—out of respect for their mystery and out of humility; it may be that to presume to name is to presume to know. But in not naming, we also name: "Yahweh" is not "God," but it is, nevertheless, a name, and it refers to God. Our brains trap us in the habit of articulation. We seem to need to reduce the world to terms we can express, even as we regret the arrogance of this necessity and hope to transcend it.

I can't see a way around the paradox; we are probably stuck with it. But we could mitigate its dangers. We could, for one thing, learn to see names not as instruments of possession or of knowing—which, in the largest sense, they can never be—but rather as invocations. Names could be seen—as they are, for instance, in many tribal cultures—as ways of calling upon the things we name: for guidance, for wisdom, for inspiration, for permission to know. Every name and every object named would then be acknowledged as sacred. This would deny the dichotomy we are always tempted to make: wildness is sacred, domesticity is profane, a distinction that leads to abuse both of wild places and of our own homes.

Wild places suffer in a secular culture such as ours when they are seen as uniquely sacred because they then become by definition irrelevant to ordinary life and thus ultimately expendable. Or they come to be regarded as antiquaries, too precious to be subjected to the ordinary vicissitudes of nature; through intensive management we freeze them in past time, as if nature itself had ceased to function with the European settlement of the continent. A wild place rigidly maintained in some ideal image of the past has been killed, just as surely as if it had been razed. Such a place, divorced from the natural processes of change and creativity, is like a mummy, preserved but not living. Or worse still, such places become totems which are defiled by the very presence of humans, totems that teach us to hate ourselves. I cannot think of any good that derives from self-hatred.

Our homes suffer too when the false dichotomy is made between the sacredness of nature and the profanity of human affairs because this distinction erodes the moral basis for tending our domestic places with love and care, mindful of the ownership that future generations rightfully have in them. What is profane is open to such abuses of land and nature as we see all around us in our domestic lives. And we cannot routinely abuse one thing without lowering our inhibitions against abusing other things. Abused land ultimately yields abused people.

The importance of wild places is not that they, unlike other places, are sacred, but that there we find, as Henry David Thoreau said, "our own limits transgressed." We confront in wild places evidence of powers greater than our own; this evidence humbles us, and in humility is the beginning of spirituality. Wildness matters not because it alone is sacred but because it arouses in us the sense of sanctity that makes visible the sacredness of everything else in life.

As I sat in the shadows along the bank of Washington Creek, a cow moose galumphed past, headed downstream. I concentrated for a few minutes on trying to see the scene as I thought the moose might, emptying my mind of words, letting only the raw sensations of sound, light, texture, and aroma in. I soon began to breath more easily. I felt the tension draining out of my weary muscles. Then I fell into a kind of trance, somewhere between waking and sleeping, completely at peace.

Later, a psychologist taught me self-hypnosis. I had no idea what to expect. "Think of a place where you felt at peace," she said. In a soft, soothing voice, she led me back to the bank of Washington Creek. I watched again the water flowing up and down the stream, heard the splashing moose, felt again the tranquility that came when I experienced the world from a moose's point of view.

I have returned to Washington Creek and Isle Royale many times since without ever leaving my wicker reading chair. When I go there, I retreat into the wildness of my own brain, transcending the limits of living in a world of words or of my own kind alone and reveling in the grace of the wild.

PAUL GRUCHOW is a freelance writer and farm owner living in Northfield, Minnesota. He has authored five previous books, including *Journal of a Prairie Year* (University of Minnesota Press, 1985), *The Necessity of Empty Places* (St. Martin's Press, 1988), and *Grass Roots* (Milkweed Editions, 1995), and published hundreds of articles, essays, and reviews in periodicals such as *Nature Conservancy*, the *Hungry Mind Review*, and the *Utne Reader*. He teaches English at Concordia College in Moorhead, Minnesota, and is a frequent lecturer and speaker on rural issues and literature.

Interior design by Will Powers
Typeset in Trump Mediaeval
by Stanton Publication Services, Inc.
Printed on acid-free Liberty paper
by Quebecor Printing

What Makes Pornography "Sexy"?
John Stoltenberg

Testimony:
Writers of the West Speak On Behalf of Utah Wilderness
Compiled by Steve Trimble
and Terry Tempest Williams